Mastering Legal Language

A Comprehensive Guide for Law Students and Lawyers

Dhananjay Modgalya

BHARAT APEX PUBLISHERS

Published by Bharat Apex Publishers in 2025

ISBN Paperback: 978-93-6679-782-3

ISBN eBook: 978-93-6679-436-5

1st edition 2025

Published by :
Bharat Apex Publishers
Website: www.bharatapexpublisher.com

Dedication

Dedicated to the aspiring legal minds, who navigate the intricacies of language to bring clarity and justice.

Epigraph

The power of law lies not in force,
but in the precision of language.

To master the language of law is to
master the art of clarity, persuasion, and justice.

Content

Acknowledgements ... vii

Preface ... ix

Chapter 1: Foundations of Legal Vocabulary ... 1

Chapter 2: Legal Systems and Courts ... 11

Chapter 3: Parties and Roles in Legal Cases ... 23

Chapter 4: Filing a Case: Understanding Pleadings ... 33

Chapter 5: Trial Terminology ... 43

Chapter 6: Judgment and Appeals ... 55

Chapter 7: Constitutional Law Vocabulary ... 67

Chapter 8: Contract Law Vocabulary ... 79

Chapter 9: Tort Law Terminology ... 89

Chapter 10: Procedural Law Vocabulary ... 99

Chapter 11: The Language of Evidence ... 111

Chapter 12: Administrative and Regulatory Law Vocabulary 121

Chapter 13: Property Law Vocabulary ... 133

Chapter 14: Business and Corporate Law Terms ... 145

Chapter 15: Criminal Law Terminology ... 157

Chapter 16: Criminal Procedure Vocabulary ... 167

Chapter 17: Mastering Legal Writing Vocabulary ... 177

Chapter 18: The Language of Legal Communication 187

Chapter 19: Latin Phrases Every Lawyer Should Know......... 197

Chapter 20: Legal Maxims and Their Application.................. 207

Glossary of Important Legal Terms 217

List Of Commonly Used Legal Maxims 223

Annexure: Expanding Legal Vocabulary 229

BONUS 231

About the Author... 233

List of Cited Cases 238

Acknowledgements

I express gratitude to the cosmic existence, the Rishis, deities, divine powers, and all beings for their guidance and support in the creation of this work.

I bow to the infinite cosmos, the vast ocean of existence that sustains all.

To the ancient Rishis whose wisdom guides us, and to the Devas who bless us with light.

To the primordial Shakti, the eternal Brahman, and the essence of all creation, I offer my salutations.

May the one who awakens me from within, the cosmic soul, be ever revered.

With deep reverence, I offer my salutations to the Sun, the giver of life, and the Moon, the guide of emotions.

To Sarasvati, the goddess of wisdom, and to the Gurus who impart the truth.

To my ancestors, my parents, my friends, and all beings who have shaped my path.

I bow with gratitude, acknowledging their blessings and grace in every step I take.

सर्वेषां भूतभावानां च रत्नाकरस्त्वं जगत्त्रयम्।
ऋषीणां देवतानां च प्रणम्य दिव्यसंपदाम्॥

आदिशक्तिं परं ब्रह्म सकलां प्रकृतिं नमः।
यो मां प्रबोधयन्नित्यं तस्मै सर्वात्मने नमः॥

नमः सूर्यमुखं ज्योतिः चन्द्रार्केन्दुसमानिधिम्।
वेदवाणीं सरस्वत्याः गुरुभ्यः शान्तिदायिनाम्॥

माता पिता सखायश्च सर्वे जनाः शुभावहाः।
तदनुग्रहवन्दनं समर्पयामि भावतः॥

Preface

The corridors of law schools are filled with a unique energy, a mix of ambition, uncertainty, and an overwhelming desire to make sense of the vast world of legal principles, cases, and jargon. As I walked into my first class over a decade ago, with my brand-new textbooks and a mind buzzing with excitement, I had no idea what lay ahead. The thought of becoming a lawyer felt both thrilling and daunting. Like most young law students, I believed that once I memorized the doctrines, learned the case laws, and studied the statutes, the legal world would start to make sense.

But I was wrong.

Becoming a lawyer is not just about knowing the law. It's about understanding the language of law, the words, phrases, and maxims that breathe life into legal principles. In those early years, every word in a legal document seemed like a mountain to climb. What is **"stare decisis"**? What's the difference between **"actus reus"** and **"mens rea"**? Why do lawyers constantly throw around Latin phrases as if they're casting spells? Like every aspiring lawyer, I struggled, fumbling through legal textbooks, asking professors endless questions, and looking at case law with a sense of awe, fear, and frustration.

Yet, slowly but surely, things began to change. With each class, each case study, each late-night session pouring over judicial opinions, I began to decipher the language of law. The seemingly cryptic Latin terms began to make sense, the heavy phrases no longer scared me, and soon, I found myself not just studying the law but engaging with it. It was during these moments of clarity that I realized, mastery of legal vocabulary is the key to truly understanding and practicing law. It's what separates students from advocates, rookies from experts.

Over the years, as I transitioned from law student to junior associate, from junior associate to lead counsel, and finally to an experienced lawyer with over 11 years of practice, I realized one universal truth: law is a language. It's a way of thinking and communicating that, once mastered, becomes the most powerful tool in a lawyer's arsenal. Every motion filed, every argument made, every case won, boils down to how well a lawyer can wield the language of law.

I've seen firsthand how law students and even new lawyers can struggle with this. The first time I stepped into a courtroom, I felt the weight of my inexperience. Despite years of rigorous study, I wasn't fully prepared for the practical reality of legal terminology in action. I vividly remember a senior lawyer once telling me, "It's not just about knowing the law, but about knowing how to speak the law." That moment transformed my approach to law forever. Legal language is not about impressing others with jargon, but about clarity, precision, and, most importantly, persuasion.

That's why I wrote this book.

"Mastering Legal Language" is born out of my own journey, from a confused law student trying to grasp Latin phrases, to a seasoned lawyer who now understands the nuances and power behind each legal term. This book is designed to bridge the gap between legal theory and practical application. It's not just a dictionary of terms; it's a guide that takes you through the real-world application of legal vocabulary, through case studies, practical examples, and interactive exercises.

I’ve seen far too many promising law students struggle because they couldn’t confidently navigate the vocabulary that underpins their field. This book aims to change that. It’s written for the student who is eager to learn, the new lawyer who is ready to practice, and even the seasoned professional who seeks to sharpen their tools.

What makes this book different is its emphasis on **understanding**, not memorizing. Anyone can look up a legal term, but this book is about embedding that term in your thinking, so when you see **“res ipsa loquitur”**, you not only know what it means, but you understand how to argue it in court. When you encounter **“mens rea”** in a criminal case, you’ll know how to link it to **actus reus** and form a compelling argument. From **contract law** to **criminal procedure**, this book covers the essentials and offers you a deeper, more intuitive connection to legal language.

My goal is to give you the tools that I wish I had when I started, tools that will save you hours of confusion, countless Google searches, and the frustration of feeling out of place in legal discussions. More importantly, I want to equip you with the confidence to walk into any legal setting, whether it's a classroom, a boardroom, or a courtroom, knowing you can hold your own.

Looking back, if there’s one thing that I’ve learned after 11 years of practice, it’s that mastery is not about knowing everything, it’s about knowing the right things well. This book focuses on that very idea. It will give you the right legal language to thrive in the demanding world of law.

So, whether you're just beginning your journey or are somewhere along the path, I hope this book becomes your guide and companion in mastering the language of law. Because when you can speak the law with confidence and clarity, the doors to success open wide, and the journey ahead becomes that much clearer.

Welcome to **"Mastering Legal Language."** Let's start this journey together.

"The law is not a black-and-white world. It's full of grey areas, nuances, and interpretations. But once you understand its language, you can see its shades of grey more clearly, and more importantly, use them to your advantage."

With love and gratitude,

Dhananjay Modgalya

(धनंजय मुद्गल्य)

मकर संक्रांति, 14.01.2025

More learning awaits you at website: www.svabhava.com

ॐ पूर्णमदः पूर्णमिदं पूर्णात्पूर्णमुदच्यते ।

पूर्णस्य पूर्णमादाय पूर्णमेवावशिष्यते ॥

ॐ शांतिः शांतिः शांतिः ॥

oṃ pūrṇamadaḥ pūrṇamidaṃ pūrṇātpūrṇamudacyate |

pūrṇasya pūrṇamādāya pūrṇamevāvaśiṣyate ||

oṃ śāṃtiḥ śāṃtiḥ śāṃtiḥ ||

Chapter 1: Foundations of Legal Vocabulary

"Law is not a mere collection of rules, but a profound engagement with the truth. Every term, every phrase, has the power to shape justice, and the wise lawyer knows that language is not just a tool, it is the foundation of the law."

\- **Nani Palkhivala**

The Language That Shapes Justice

Imagine standing in a courtroom, surrounded by men and women in black robes, the tension palpable as words are exchanged, not casually, but with the weight of decisions that could change lives. These words, **law**, **right**, **duty**, **liability**, are more than vocabulary; they are the very mechanisms of justice. The power of language in the legal arena is immense, and mastering it is your first step in becoming a lawyer of influence, intellect, and integrity.

Legal language, often seen as daunting, is your most potent weapon. Each term is loaded with centuries of interpretation, precedent, and nuance. In this chapter, we will break down the essential elements of legal vocabulary, those that will form the bedrock of your understanding of law. As you grasp these terms, you will not only learn to speak the language of law but also to think in it. This thinking, this shaping of your mind around legal concepts, will empower you in ways you cannot yet imagine.

"A lawyer's time and advice are his stock in trade."

\- **Abraham Lincoln**

Before diving into the cases, the complexities of legal thought, you must first understand the words that make up the law. In this chapter, we will cover essential terms such as **law**, **right**, **duty**, **liability**, and **jurisdiction**, along with Latin phrases like ***mens rea***, ***habeas corpus***, and ***de jure***, which breathe life into legal principles. Through the lens of case law and precedents, you will see how these terms are not static but dynamic, constantly interpreted and reinterpreted by courts.

Law: More Than Just Rules

At its core, **law** is a system of rules that governs a society. But law is more than a set of instructions; it is the embodiment of societal values, ethics, and collective wisdom. To be a lawyer is to participate in the creation and interpretation of this system. Law is fluid, evolving with the times, shaped by precedents that are laid down case by case.

Consider the landmark case of **Kesavananda Bharati v. State of Kerala** (1973). This Indian Supreme Court case is a testament to the evolving nature of law. The case was primarily about the extent of Parliament's power to amend the Constitution. It established the "basic structure doctrine," a principle that while Parliament can amend most parts of the Constitution, it cannot alter its basic structure. Through this judgment, we see that the law is not rigid; it grows and adapts, guided by the interpretations of the courts.

The term "law" in this context becomes not just a rule but a reflection of the collective will, a safeguard for the future of democracy. The lawyer, in this case, Nani Palkhivala, demonstrated how law serves as both a sword and a shield, protecting the Constitution from being dismantled, even by the highest authority in the land.

Case Study: Kesavananda Bharati v. State of Kerala

In this case, Kesavananda Bharati, a religious leader, challenged the Kerala government's land reforms that impacted the monastery's property. The case soon evolved into a debate on whether Parliament had the power to alter fundamental rights. The court's majority judgment introduced the concept of the basic structure, meaning that certain principles of the Constitution, like rule of law, separation of powers, and judicial review, could not be amended. The law in this sense became a living organism, embodying more than just rules, it carried values that must be upheld for future generations.

This case teaches us that understanding the concept of **law** is not just about knowing statutes or acts. It's about grasping the spirit that drives the rules, knowing that every piece of legislation is part of a larger framework designed to balance power and protect individual freedoms.

Right: The Power to Act

Rights are the cornerstone of justice. In legal terms, a right is an entitlement granted by law. These can be constitutional, statutory, or contractual. Rights give individuals the power to act or refrain from acting in certain ways. The significance of rights in the legal framework is vast, they form the foundation of civil liberties and human dignity.

One of the most important cases in Indian legal history concerning rights is **Maneka Gandhi v. Union of India** (1978). In this case, the petitioner, Maneka Gandhi, was issued a passport by the Government of India, but it was later impounded without giving her any reason. The case reached the Supreme Court, where the main issue was whether the procedure prescribed by law for restricting someone's fundamental rights (in this case, the right to travel) was just, fair, and reasonable.

Case Study: Maneka Gandhi v. Union of India

In its judgment, the Supreme Court expanded the interpretation of Article 21 of the Indian Constitution, which guarantees the right to life and personal liberty. The Court held that any procedure established by law to deprive a person of their rights must be fair, just, and reasonable, and not arbitrary. This case transformed the understanding of personal liberty in India, broadening the scope of rights under Article 21.

This case reminds us that **rights** are not static, they grow with society's understanding of justice and fairness. To be an effective lawyer, you must understand not only what rights exist but how they can be argued, expanded, and protected through the law.

Duty: The Counterbalance to Rights

Where there are rights, there are also **duties**. A duty in law is a legal obligation imposed on an individual or entity to act in a certain way. Duties often function as the counterbalance to rights, where one person holds a right, another holds a corresponding duty to respect that right.

For example, the right to property means that others have the duty not to infringe upon that property. Duties are not only imposed on individuals but also on governments and institutions. A compelling case that illustrates the concept of duty is **Donoghue v. Stevenson** (1932), a UK case that laid the foundation for modern negligence law.

Case Study: Donoghue v. Stevenson

In this landmark case, the plaintiff, Mrs. Donoghue, consumed a bottle of ginger beer that contained a decomposed snail. She sued the manufacturer, Mr. Stevenson, for negligence. The court ruled in her favor, stating that the manufacturer owed a duty of care to the ultimate consumer, even though there was no direct contract between them. This case established the famous "neighbor principle", the idea that one must take reasonable care to avoid acts or omissions that could foreseeably injure one's "neighbor."

The ruling emphasized that the concept of **duty** is critical in determining liability, especially in tort law. It reinforces that individuals and corporations have duties toward others in society, and failing in those duties can result in legal consequences.

Liability: Responsibility for One's Actions

Liability is the legal responsibility for one's actions or omissions. It arises when someone breaches their legal duty and causes harm or injury to another party. In both civil and criminal cases, establishing liability is key to determining whether the person responsible should compensate the victim or be punished for the wrongdoing.

A powerful example of how **liability** functions in criminal law is the **Nirbhaya Rape Case** (2012), formally known as **Mukesh & Anr. v. State for NCT of Delhi & Ors**. The brutal gang rape and murder of a young woman in Delhi shocked the nation and led to widespread protests demanding justice. The perpetrators were held liable for their actions under multiple sections of the Indian Penal Code, including sections related to rape and murder.

Case Study: Nirbhaya Rape Case

In this case, the court imposed the harshest penalties on the defendants, including the death sentence, as their actions not only violated the victim's rights but also breached the duty of care that every citizen owes to another human being. The liability here was both criminal and moral, the defendants were held accountable for their heinous acts under the strictest legal standards.

This case teaches us that **liability** goes beyond merely identifying wrongs, it is about ensuring that those responsible are made to answer for their actions in a court of law. Whether it's compensating the injured in a civil suit or punishing criminals, liability is the backbone of justice.

Jurisdiction: The Power to Hear and Decide

Jurisdiction refers to the authority of a court to hear and decide a case. Without jurisdiction, no court has the power to pass judgment on a legal issue. Understanding jurisdiction is crucial for young lawyers because it affects where and how a case can be tried.

A profound example of the importance of jurisdiction is the **Union Carbide Corporation v. Union of India** (Bhopal Gas Tragedy, 1989). In this case, the Union of India sued Union Carbide Corporation (UCC) in U.S. courts, seeking damages for the thousands of deaths and injuries caused by the release of toxic gas in Bhopal, India. However, the U.S. court dismissed the case, ruling that India was the appropriate jurisdiction for the trial.

Case Study: Union Carbide Corporation v. Union of India

The court in the U.S. held that India had more significant ties to the case, and thus, the Indian courts were the correct jurisdiction for the lawsuit. This led to a landmark settlement in the Indian courts, where UCC agreed to pay $470 million in compensation to the victims of the tragedy.

This case underlines the concept of **jurisdiction**, that legal authority must be carefully determined based on factors such as location, parties involved, and the nature of the case. Understanding where and how a court has the right to hear a case is as crucial as understanding the facts of the case itself.

Latin Phrases: The Timeless Language of Law

Latin phrases remain deeply embedded in legal language, often serving as shorthand for complex legal principles. These phrases have been passed down through centuries of legal thought and continue to shape modern law.

Mens Rea and Actus Reus

In criminal law, two Latin phrases are central to determining guilt: **mens rea** (guilty mind) and **actus reus** (guilty act). These phrases capture the essence of criminal liability, both the intention and the action must be present for a crime to be complete.

State of West Bengal v. Shew Mangal Singh (1981), where the Indian Supreme Court emphasized that criminal liability requires both ***mens rea*** and ***actus reus***. In this case, the accused was acquitted because, although the act had occurred, there was no evidence of intention (***mens rea***).

Habeas Corpus

The phrase ***habeas corpus*** means "you shall have the body" and is a legal remedy to challenge unlawful detention. One of the most famous cases involving ***habeas corpus*** in India is **ADM Jabalpur v. Shivkant Shukla** (1976), where the Supreme Court ruled that during the Emergency, the right to seek ***habeas corpus*** could be suspended. This controversial decision was widely criticized for undermining fundamental rights.

Years later, the decision was overturned, and ***habeas corpus*** was reaffirmed as a critical protection against state power, ensuring that individuals cannot be detained without legal justification.

De Jure and De Facto

The terms ***de jure*** (by law) and ***de facto*** (in fact) are used to distinguish between what is legally recognized and what exists in reality. In the case of **Keshav Singh v. Speaker, Legislative Assembly, UP** (1965), the Supreme Court dealt with the issue of whether an assembly's privileges could override an individual's ***de jure*** rights. The court held that ***de jure*** rights enshrined in the Constitution could not be overridden by ***de facto*** practices of the assembly, reinforcing the supremacy of law.

Exercises and Practical Applications

By now, you have grasped the foundations of legal vocabulary, but knowledge becomes power only when applied. Below are some exercises designed to deepen your understanding and prepare you for practical applications of these terms in real-world legal scenarios.

Exercise 1: Identifying Legal Terms in Context

Read the following case summary and identify where the terms **liability**, **right**, and **jurisdiction** are applied:

"A multinational corporation was sued by a local government for environmental damages caused by industrial pollution. The case was initially filed in the U.S., but the court ruled that the jurisdiction lay in the country where the harm occurred. The court ultimately found the corporation liable for violating environmental regulations, and the government asserted its right to compensation for the damage caused."

Exercise 2: Using Legal Terms in Sentences

Write sentences using the following terms:

- **Duty**
- **Habeas Corpus**
- **Mens Rea**
- **Plaintiff**

Exercise 3: Case Law Analysis

Review the case **Maneka Gandhi v. Union of India** (1978). Discuss how the court expanded the interpretation of personal liberty under Article 21. How did the terms **right** and **duty** play a pivotal role in the judgment?

The terms you have learned in this chapter are not just words; they are the keys that unlock the deeper understanding of law and justice. As you move forward in your legal education, these foundational concepts will shape the way you think, argue, and navigate the legal landscape.

To be a great lawyer, you must not only know these terms but master their use in every case, every brief, and every conversation. The law is not static, it lives and evolves with every interpretation and precedent set by the courts. As you continue to build your legal vocabulary, remember that each term is a tool, and in your hands, it has the power to shape the future of justice.

"Justice must not only be done, but must also be seen to be done."

\- **Lord Hewart, R v. Sussex Justices, ex parte McCarthy (1924)**

Chapter 2: Legal Systems and Courts

"A court is not only the stage where laws are performed; it is the very crucible where justice is forged. The system we adopt is the language in which justice speaks."

\- **Justice H.R. Khanna**

The Foundation Beneath the Law

When you first walk into a courtroom, it is not just the physical structure that commands attention, the towering bench, the watchful eyes of the judge, but the invisible architecture that underpins it: the legal system. Whether you find yourself in a common law court in India or a civil law court in France, the language of justice is shaped by the legal system you are part of. And just as a skilled orator must master the subtleties of language, a great lawyer must understand the foundation that supports every word uttered in a court of law.

But what is this foundation? How does the legal system shape the journey of justice? Today, we will explore the two primary legal systems, common law and civil law, as well as specialized systems like statutory law and equity. We will also dive into the structure of courts, from trial courts to the highest appellate courts, where justice is debated, argued, and decided.

By the end of this chapter, you will not only understand the technical differences between legal systems, but you will also grasp how these systems influence the trajectory of justice. And as we unravel each layer, you will see that courts are not just venues for argument but sanctuaries of legal reasoning.

The Common Law System: Shaped by Precedent

Common law, also known as **case law**, is a system of law based on judicial decisions and precedents. It is one of the oldest systems of law, with roots in medieval England. In a common law system, the decisions made by higher courts create **binding precedents** that must be followed by lower courts in similar cases. It is often said that common law is "judge-made law" because it evolves through the decisions of judges, rather than through statutes or legislative bodies.

Evolution of Common Law Through Precedents

One of the key aspects of common law is the principle of **stare decisis**, a Latin phrase meaning "to stand by things decided." This principle ensures that courts follow precedents to maintain consistency and fairness. In a way, the legal profession is a dialogue between the present and the past, a conversation between current judges and the rulings of those who came before.

In **Kesavananda Bharati v. State of Kerala** (1973), the Indian Supreme Court, while defining the limits of Parliament's amending power, upheld the basic structure doctrine. This doctrine holds that certain parts of the Indian Constitution, such as the rule of law and judicial review, cannot be amended. Although not a common law case per se, the ruling illustrated how legal principles evolve through judicial interpretation, drawing from past precedents and judicial wisdom. The basic structure doctrine now stands as an essential precedent in Indian constitutional law, one that future cases must adhere to.

The importance of precedent can be further illustrated by looking at **Brown v. Board of Education** (1954) in the United States. This landmark case overturned the infamous **Plessy v. Ferguson** (1896), which had established the doctrine of "separate but equal." Through the principle of stare decisis, the U.S. Supreme Court ruled that racial segregation in public schools was unconstitutional, setting a binding precedent that rippled across the entire legal system. This decision reshaped American society, underscoring the role of courts in not just interpreting but actively crafting the law through precedent.

Case Study: Vishaka v. State of Rajasthan

To understand how precedents shape the law in a practical sense, we turn to the Indian case of **Vishaka v. State of Rajasthan** (1997). In this case, a woman working with a social welfare organization was raped by her colleagues. There were no clear statutory laws regarding sexual harassment in the workplace at the time. The Supreme Court of India stepped in, drawing from international conventions and principles, to issue guidelines for workplace sexual harassment. These became known as the **Vishaka Guidelines**.

This decision was monumental not only because it filled a legal gap but because it set a precedent that was binding on all workplaces across India. The Vishaka case is a powerful example of how common law evolves, where courts do not merely interpret statutes but also create enforceable guidelines in the absence of legislation.

Common Law in Practice: A Dynamic, Evolving System

The beauty of the common law system is that it allows for flexibility and evolution. Judges in common law jurisdictions have the power to adapt legal principles to new circumstances. But this flexibility is tempered by the weight of precedent, ensuring that changes in the law are thoughtful and incremental.

As a lawyer working within a common law system, you will find that your role often involves researching previous decisions to support your arguments. Precedents are the compass that guides legal reasoning, and by understanding them, you can predict how a court may rule in your case. In every argument, you are standing on the shoulders of those who came before you.

The Civil Law System: Rooted in Codification

While common law thrives on precedents, **civil law** is a system based on comprehensive legal codes and statutes. This legal system is primarily found in Europe and countries influenced by European legal traditions, such as France and Germany. Unlike common law, where judicial decisions play a dominant role, civil law relies on written codes that provide detailed rules for judges to follow.

Codification: The Backbone of Civil Law

Civil law traces its origins to the **Roman legal system**, which emphasized codification. The **Napoleonic Code** (Code Civil), established in 1804, is perhaps the most famous civil law code and serves as the foundation for many civil law systems around the world. In a civil law system, judges apply the law as written in the code. Their primary task is not to interpret the law in light of previous decisions but to apply it strictly to the facts before them.

In **France**, for example, a judge handling a contract dispute would refer directly to the civil code, which provides specific rules for contract formation, breach, and remedies. The goal of civil law is to create a system that is clear, predictable, and consistent. Unlike common law, where past cases may sway a judge's interpretation, civil law judges have less discretion because they are bound by the statutory language.

Case Study: Indian Penal Code (IPC)

Although India is primarily a common law jurisdiction, its **Indian Penal Code (IPC)** is a prime example of codified law that aligns with civil law traditions. The IPC, drafted in 1860, outlines specific offenses and prescribes punishments for those offenses. For example, Section 300 defines murder, while Section 302 prescribes the punishment for it. Judges in India apply the IPC directly when deciding criminal cases.

A notable case involving the IPC is **State of Maharashtra v. Afzal Khan** (1997). In this case, the accused was charged under Section 302 of the IPC for committing murder. The court applied the clear language of the IPC to convict the accused, without needing to rely on previous judicial decisions. This case underscores the way that codified law functions in practice: judges apply the statute directly to the facts, offering a more predictable and less discretionary form of justice.

In this way, civil law's reliance on codification offers a system that is, at its heart, concerned with predictability. For a young lawyer, this means a deep familiarity with the code is essential. In the civil law system, your power comes from your ability to know the statute inside out, and to apply its provisions to your client's case.

Differences Between Common Law and Civil Law

While common law and civil law systems share the same goal, justice, their approaches are strikingly different. A lawyer trained in the common law system must rely heavily on case law, researching precedents and building arguments based on previous judgments. In contrast, a lawyer in a civil law jurisdiction spends more time analyzing statutes and understanding the intricacies of the code.

In **Dahlia v. Four Millbank Nominees** (1978), a UK common law case, the court had to determine whether specific actions constituted an acceptance of a contract offer, considering prior judgments on the matter. In contrast, in a civil law country like Germany, the judge would look directly at the **German Civil Code** (BGB) to resolve a similar dispute.

For young lawyers, understanding the differences between these systems is crucial. While common law offers flexibility and evolution through judicial decisions, civil law provides predictability and consistency through codified statutes. Both systems are powerful, but they require different skills and approaches.

Statutory Law: When Legislation Speaks

Statutory law refers to laws passed by a legislative body, such as Parliament or Congress. Unlike common law, where judicial decisions create binding precedents, statutory law is written law. When a statute is clear, courts must apply it as written. However, when a statute is ambiguous, courts may be called upon to interpret its meaning, often using principles of **statutory interpretation**.

The Role of Statutory Law in the Legal System

Statutory law plays a central role in all legal systems, whether common law or civil law. While common law evolves through judicial decisions, statutory law is created through a democratic process. Legislators draft statutes, and courts are responsible for applying and interpreting them.

In **Shayara Bano v. Union of India** (2017), a landmark case in India, the Supreme Court ruled that the practice of **triple talaq** (instant divorce) was unconstitutional. This case led to the passing of the **Muslim Women (Protection of Rights on Marriage) Act, 2019**, which codified the court's ruling into statutory law. The act criminalized the practice of triple talaq and established clear legal remedies for women affected by it.

This case demonstrates how statutory law can evolve in response to judicial decisions. Courts interpret the law, and legislatures codify those interpretations, ensuring that the law reflects the values of society.

Case Study: Roe v. Wade and the Right to Privacy

In **Roe v. Wade** (1973), the U.S. Supreme Court ruled that women have a constitutional right to privacy, which includes the right to choose whether to have an abortion. This decision was based on the interpretation of the **Due Process Clause** of the 14th Amendment, but it also led to statutory changes. After the ruling, several states passed laws protecting or restricting access to abortion, showing how judicial interpretations can influence statutory law.

While the decision in **Roe v. Wade** was controversial, it is an example of how courts and legislatures interact. The courts may interpret the law, but ultimately, it is up to the legislature to pass statutes that reflect the will of the people.

Equity: When Fairness Demands a Remedy

Equity is a branch of law that developed alongside common law to provide remedies when the strict application of common law rules would result in injustice. In common law systems, equity serves as a **corrective** mechanism, offering relief in cases where the law does not provide an adequate remedy.

The Role of Equity in the Legal System

Equity is a powerful tool for lawyers, as it allows courts to go beyond the letter of the law to achieve a just outcome. For example, in cases involving breach of contract, a court may award **specific performance**, a remedy that requires the breaching party to fulfill their contractual obligations, rather than simply awarding damages.

A well-known example of equity in action is the **Maxims of Equity**, such as "Equity will not suffer a wrong to be without a remedy" and "He who comes into equity must come with clean hands." These principles guide courts in deciding whether equitable relief is appropriate.

In **Central London Property Trust Ltd v. High Trees House Ltd** (1947), the UK Court of Appeal applied the equitable principle of **promissory estoppel**. In this case, the landlords of High Trees House agreed to reduce the rent during World War II because the building was only partially occupied. After the war, the landlords attempted to claim the full rent retroactively. The court held that, based on the principle of promissory estoppel, the landlords were estopped from claiming the full rent for the wartime period because they had promised the tenants a reduction, and the tenants had relied on that promise.

This case illustrates how equity can prevent parties from acting unjustly, even when the law might otherwise allow it. Equity is not just about applying rules; it is about achieving fairness in the face of rigid legal principles.

Case Study: M.C. Mehta v. Union of India

In environmental law, equity plays a crucial role in ensuring justice. In the case of **M.C. Mehta v. Union of India** (1987), the Supreme Court of India applied the **polluter pays principle**, an equitable doctrine that requires polluters to bear the costs of environmental damage they cause. The case arose out of the **Bhopal Gas Tragedy**, where thousands of people were killed or injured due to the release of toxic gas from a pesticide plant.

In its ruling, the court held that Union Carbide Corporation, the company responsible for the plant, was liable for compensating the victims. This decision was not just based on statutory law, but on the equitable principle that those who harm the environment should be held accountable for the costs of their actions.

The Court System: From Trial Courts to the Supreme Court

The structure of the court system is integral to the administration of justice. Courts are divided into different levels, with **trial courts** handling the initial proceedings of a case, **appellate courts** reviewing the decisions of lower courts, and **Supreme Courts** serving as the final authority on legal matters.

Trial Courts: Where Justice Begins

A **trial court** is where a case begins. Here, facts are established, evidence is presented, and witnesses are called. Trial courts are often referred to as courts of **first instance**, because they are the first venue where a case is heard.

In the **Nirbhaya Rape Case** (2012), formally known as **Mukesh & Anr. v. State for NCT of Delhi & Ors.**, the trial court played a crucial role in hearing testimony from witnesses, reviewing forensic evidence, and determining the guilt of the accused. This case, involving the brutal gang rape and murder of a young woman in Delhi, shocked the nation and led to widespread protests calling for justice.

The trial court found the accused guilty and imposed the death sentence, a decision that was later upheld by the appellate courts. This case illustrates how trial courts serve as the foundation for justice, where facts are first established, and judgments are rendered based on those facts.

Appellate Courts: Reviewing Lower Court Decisions

An **appellate court** reviews the decisions of lower courts to ensure that the law was applied correctly. Appellate courts do not typically re-examine the facts of the case but focus on whether the trial court made any errors in applying the law.

In the case of **Arun G. Hegde v. State of Karnataka** (2019), the Karnataka High Court reviewed a lower court's decision in a criminal case. The appellate court examined whether the trial court had correctly interpreted the law in convicting the accused. Ultimately, the appellate court found that the lower court had erred in its interpretation and overturned the conviction.

This case highlights the importance of appellate courts in ensuring that justice is administered fairly and that the law is applied consistently across different cases. Appellate courts serve as a safeguard against legal errors and help maintain the integrity of the judicial system.

Supreme Courts: The Final Arbiter

At the top of the judicial hierarchy is the **Supreme Court**. The Supreme Court is the highest court in a country, and its decisions are final and binding on all lower courts. In many countries, including India and the United States, the Supreme Court has the power of **judicial review**, allowing it to strike down laws that are unconstitutional.

One of the most famous examples of the Supreme Court exercising this power is **Marbury v. Madison** (1803) in the United States. In this case, the U.S. Supreme Court, under Chief Justice John Marshall, established the principle of judicial review, giving the court the authority to invalidate laws that conflict with the U.S. Constitution. This ruling cemented the role of the Supreme Court as the ultimate guardian of the Constitution and the final arbiter of legal disputes.

In India, the Supreme Court plays a similar role, with cases like **K.S. Puttaswamy v. Union of India** (2017), which recognized the right to privacy as a fundamental right under the Indian Constitution. The Supreme Court of India's decisions in cases like Puttaswamy have far-reaching implications, not only shaping the law but also influencing public policy and individual rights.

The Intersection of Systems and Courts

As you have seen, the legal system is a complex network where different principles, precedents, and codes come together to shape justice. Whether it is the flexibility of common law, the predictability of civil law, the authority of statutory law, or the fairness of equity, each system plays a vital role in ensuring that justice is not just done, but seen to be done.

The courts, from trial courts to the Supreme Court, serve as the stages where this complex interplay unfolds. The lawyer's task, then, is not merely to know the law but to understand the system within which that law operates. When you stand before a judge, it is not just the facts of the case that matter, it is the system that governs those facts, the precedents that guide decisions, and the codes that lay down the rules.

To be a great lawyer, you must master both the language of the law and the systems that speak through it. And in this mastery, you will find not just success, but the profound satisfaction that comes from standing at the very heart of justice.

"The life of the law has not been logic; it has been experience."
- **Justice Oliver Wendell Holmes, The Common Law**

Exercises and Practical Applications

1. **Case Law Analysis**:

Choose a landmark case (such as **Brown v. Board of Education** or **Kesavananda Bharati v. State of Kerala**) and identify how the legal system (common law, statutory law, or equity) influenced the final decision. Discuss how the court's decision shaped the legal landscape.

2. **Court Structure Exercise**:

   Create a flowchart of the court system in your country, from trial courts to the Supreme Court. Identify which types of cases are heard at each level and what kinds of decisions each court can make.

3. **Practical Application**:

   Imagine you are representing a client in a common law system. Research and cite two precedents that would support your client's case. Write a brief explaining how these precedents apply to your client's situation and why the court should rule in their favor based on these past decisions.

4. **Statutory Law Interpretation**:

   Find a statute from the **Indian Penal Code** or another legal code and analyze its language. Write a short paragraph explaining how a judge might interpret this statute in light of an ambiguous case.

By engaging with these exercises, you will deepen your understanding of the legal systems and courts that shape the law and begin to think like a lawyer, ready to navigate the intricate maze of justice.

Chapter 3: Parties and Roles in Legal Cases

"The duty of a lawyer is to represent their client to the best of their ability, but also to ensure that justice is done. Sometimes, these two duties are in conflict, and that is where true legal skill and ethical judgment come into play."

- **Lord Denning**

The Players on the Stage of Justice

When a case comes before a court, it is much like a grand theater. There is a story unfolding, with facts and evidence forming the plot, but the real drama is shaped by the actors, the litigants, lawyers, judges, and various other participants who play their roles. Each party holds a key responsibility, and their roles are not arbitrary. They are defined by law, tradition, and the profound goal of achieving justice.

In any legal case, the success or failure of the arguments often hinges on understanding the dynamics between these parties. Whether you are the **plaintiff**, the one bringing the suit, or the **defendant**, the one who stands accused or is defending against a claim, the role you occupy shapes the strategy, the language, and ultimately, the outcome of the case. Equally critical are the judges, lawyers, appellants, and respondents, each contributing to the resolution of disputes that reach the courts.

In this chapter, we will dissect these roles and explore how they fit within the structure of legal proceedings. We will draw upon real-life cases to illuminate how the parties and professionals involved in a case affect its trajectory. As you read, remember: a legal case is never just about facts, it's about the people who bring those facts to life and how they wield the roles assigned to them.

Key Parties in a Legal Case

At the heart of any legal case are the **parties**, those who have a direct stake in the outcome of the matter. Typically, these include the **plaintiff** and the **defendant** in civil cases or the **prosecution** and **defendant** in criminal cases. Understanding these basic roles is critical because every legal action, regardless of its complexity, begins with one party seeking a remedy and another resisting that remedy.

The Plaintiff: Initiating the Legal Action

The **plaintiff** is the individual or entity that brings a case before the court, seeking legal redress. In civil litigation, the plaintiff is typically the party that feels wronged and seeks compensation or another remedy for the harm suffered. The plaintiff must establish their **standing**, the legal right to bring the action, and prove the **burden of proof**.

Take, for example, the case of **Balwant Singh v. Commissioner of Police** (1985), where the plaintiff, Balwant Singh, filed a lawsuit after being unlawfully detained by the police. Singh, the plaintiff, argued that his detention violated his fundamental rights under the Indian Constitution. The case reached the Supreme Court, where it was held that his detention was indeed unlawful, and Singh was awarded compensation for the wrongful act.

This case illustrates the importance of the plaintiff's role in initiating an action. It is the plaintiff who drives the narrative, choosing the grounds on which the case will be argued. From the moment a plaintiff files a suit, they carry the responsibility of convincing the court that they have suffered harm and deserve relief.

The Defendant: Protecting Against Allegations

On the other side stands the **defendant**, the party against whom the legal action is brought. In civil cases, the defendant must respond to the plaintiff's allegations, often by denying liability or presenting **affirmative defenses** to counter the claims. In criminal cases, the defendant is accused of violating a law and faces the possibility of punishment if found guilty.

One of the most famous examples of a defendant vigorously defending their rights is the **Self-Defense Plea in the Manu Sharma Case** (Jessica Lal Murder Case, 1999). Manu Sharma, the defendant, was initially acquitted by the lower court but was later convicted by the Delhi High Court after a media outcry and public demand for justice. Sharma claimed that he was not present at the crime scene, but the court, after examining the evidence, convicted him. The role of the defendant here was to protect against the prosecution's narrative, but ultimately, it was the prosecution's well-established case that led to conviction.

In every legal case, the defendant carries a unique burden. While the plaintiff must prove the case, the defendant must strategically dismantle the plaintiff's claims, protect their interests, and often work from a defensive position, yet with the hope of securing a favorable outcome.

Case Study: Hussainara Khatoon v. State of Bihar

One of the most critical cases involving the rights of defendants is **Hussainara Khatoon v. State of Bihar** (1979), a landmark case in India that reshaped the understanding of fundamental rights, particularly for undertrials. In this case, a group of women, including Hussainara Khatoon, had been languishing in Bihar jails for extended periods without trial. The petitioners, representing the defendants (the undertrials), argued that their constitutional right to a **speedy trial** had been violated.

The Supreme Court ruled in favor of the petitioners, declaring that prolonged detention without trial was a violation of fundamental rights. This case underscored the role of the defendant in protecting their constitutional rights and highlighted the responsibility of the legal system to provide timely justice.

In this instance, the defendants were not merely passive participants; their plight became the catalyst for legal reform. The case emphasized that while defendants are often seen as being on the back foot, their rights are at the heart of the justice system.

Professional Roles in the Legal System

Beyond the parties to the case are the professionals who facilitate the legal process. These include **attorneys**, **judges**, **magistrates**, and **clerks**. Each plays a critical role in ensuring that justice is served, from advising clients to interpreting the law and delivering judgments.

The Attorney: Advocate and Advisor

In any legal proceeding, the **attorney** is the individual tasked with representing one of the parties. The role of an attorney is multifaceted: they must advocate zealously for their client while providing sound legal advice based on the merits of the case. Whether representing the plaintiff or the defendant, an attorney is often the voice that shapes the legal narrative, builds the argument, and navigates through the legal maze.

Consider the role of **Fali Nariman**, one of India's most celebrated attorneys, in the **S.R. Bommai v. Union of India** (1994) case. This case centered around the issue of **President's Rule** and the dismissal of state governments, raising questions about the federal structure of India. Nariman, representing S.R. Bommai, argued that the imposition of President's Rule in Karnataka was unconstitutional.

Nariman's meticulous arguments before the Supreme Court shaped the final judgment, which clarified that the judiciary had the power to review the imposition of President's Rule. His role as an attorney in this case exemplifies the power of advocacy. Through well-reasoned arguments, an attorney can not only win a case but also shape constitutional law for decades to come.

An attorney, therefore, is not just a hired representative; they are the intellectual engine behind the case, guiding it through the complexities of the legal system. The strength of their advocacy can turn the tide in favor of their client or shape a new legal precedent.

The Judge: The Neutral Arbiter

The **judge** is the individual tasked with ensuring that justice is delivered impartially and according to the law. While the parties and attorneys argue their case, it is the judge's role to interpret the law and apply it to the facts of the case. A judge's neutrality is paramount, as their decisions affect not only the parties involved but also the broader interpretation of law in society.

A powerful example of judicial impartiality can be seen in **Keshav Singh's Case** (1965), which involved a complex conflict between the legislative assembly's privileges and an individual's fundamental rights. In this case, Keshav Singh was imprisoned by the Uttar Pradesh Legislative Assembly for contempt of the House. The matter reached the Allahabad High Court, where Justice Nasirullah Beg ruled that while the legislature had certain privileges, they could not override the fundamental rights of individuals guaranteed by the Constitution.

This case highlighted the critical role judges play in balancing competing interests and interpreting the Constitution in a way that upholds justice. The judgment ensured that legislative privileges did not erode individual rights, a fine example of judicial responsibility.

The Magistrate: Dispensing Justice at the Grassroots

A **magistrate** is often the first point of contact in the legal system for many individuals, especially in criminal cases. Magistrates handle preliminary hearings, minor criminal offenses, and civil matters at a local level. While their powers are more limited than those of judges in higher courts, magistrates play an essential role in ensuring that justice is accessible to all, particularly at the grassroots level.

In **A. R. Antulay v. R. S. Nayak** (1988), the Bombay High Court's magistrate was involved in handling the early stages of a significant political corruption case. Antulay, a former Chief Minister of Maharashtra, was accused of misappropriating public funds. The case eventually made its way to the Supreme Court, where the court held that due process and the principles of natural justice had not been followed.

The Antulay case illustrates that even decisions made by lower courts and magistrates have far-reaching implications. The role of the magistrate in ensuring that justice is dispensed fairly at the local level cannot be underestimated. Their decisions, though often preliminary, set the stage for how a case will proceed.

The Appellants and Respondents: Revisiting the Verdict

When a party is dissatisfied with the judgment of a lower court, they may appeal the decision to a higher court. In such cases, the parties are referred to as the **appellant** and **respondent**. The **appellant** is the party that files the appeal, seeking to overturn or modify the lower court's ruling, while the **respondent** is the party that defends the original decision.

The Appellant: Seeking a Second Chance

The appellant plays a crucial role in ensuring that justice is revisited when an error in law or procedure is suspected. The right to appeal is a fundamental aspect of the legal system, providing a mechanism for correction and further interpretation of legal principles.

One of the most important cases involving the appellant's role is **Maneka Gandhi v. Union of India** (1978), where the appellant, Maneka Gandhi, challenged the government's decision to impound her passport. Gandhi argued that the government's action violated her fundamental rights under Article 21 of the Constitution (the right to life and personal liberty). The Supreme Court ruled in her favor, significantly expanding the interpretation of Article 21 to include not only physical liberty but also personal freedoms such as the right to travel.

In this case, the appellant's courage to challenge the government's actions led to a groundbreaking judgment that reshaped the landscape of Indian constitutional law. As an appellant, you are not only seeking justice for yourself but potentially paving the way for legal reform.

The Respondent: Defending the Judgment

The **respondent**, on the other hand, is tasked with defending the lower court's judgment. The respondent argues that the initial ruling was correct, and there is no need for modification or reversal.

In **State of Tamil Nadu v. K. Balu** (2017), the respondent, the State of Tamil Nadu, defended the Supreme Court's earlier decision to ban liquor shops within 500 meters of national and state highways to reduce road accidents. The liquor vendors, as appellants, sought to overturn this decision, arguing that it harmed their business. However, the respondent (the State of Tamil Nadu) successfully defended the ban, and the Supreme Court upheld the decision, emphasizing public safety over commercial interests.

The role of the respondent is equally crucial, as they must protect the integrity of the original judgment while facing challenges from the appellant. A well-argued response can preserve legal precedents and protect public policy.

Supporting Roles in the Legal Process

Beyond the primary parties and professionals, several other roles are essential to the smooth functioning of the legal system. These include **court clerks**, **paralegals**, **witnesses**, and **experts**. While these roles may not be as visible as those of the judges or attorneys, they are vital to ensuring that cases are conducted efficiently and fairly.

Court Clerks: Guardians of the Court's Administrative Machinery

Court clerks are responsible for maintaining records, filing motions, and managing the logistical aspects of a case. Their work ensures that the judicial process runs smoothly, from the initial filing to the final verdict. Though often overlooked, their role is indispensable in the legal process.

Paralegals: The Backbone of Legal Research

Paralegals assist attorneys by conducting research, drafting documents, and organizing case files. In high-profile cases like **The Ayodhya Dispute** (2019), paralegals played a crucial role in gathering historical records, legal precedents, and land documents to support the arguments presented by both parties. While the attorneys argued the case, it was the behind-the-scenes work of paralegals that helped shape the final presentation.

Witnesses and Experts: The Voice of Evidence

Witnesses, both **lay witnesses** (those who testify about facts) and **expert witnesses** (those who offer specialized knowledge), are critical to the presentation of evidence in a trial. In the **Nithari Serial Killings** case, expert forensic witnesses played a key role in presenting evidence related to DNA analysis, which ultimately helped secure the conviction of the accused.

Conclusion: Understanding Roles

Each party in a legal case, whether plaintiff, defendant, attorney, judge, or even clerk, holds a specific role with defined responsibilities. Mastering these roles is essential for any lawyer who hopes to navigate the legal system effectively. Understanding the dynamics between these roles helps shape the strategy, build the narrative, and ultimately influence the outcome of a case.

When you step into a courtroom, remember that every role contributes to the larger pursuit of justice. It is not just about winning or losing, it is about ensuring that each party plays their part in a system that seeks fairness, truth, and resolution.

"In the halls of justice, the wheels turn slowly, but grind exceedingly fine."

\- **Sun Tzu**

Exercises and Practical Applications

1. Case Role Identification:

Choose a well-known case (such as **Maneka Gandhi v. Union of India** or **Hussainara Khatoon v. State of Bihar**) and identify the key roles in the case, including the plaintiff, defendant, attorneys, and judges. Write a brief explanation of how each role influenced the outcome of the case.

2. Mock Courtroom Scenario:

Imagine you are an attorney representing a defendant in a civil case. Develop a strategy for defending against the plaintiff's claims, keeping in mind the role of the defendant and the potential defenses available. Present your strategy in a brief.

3. Appellate Brief Drafting:

Write an appellate brief for a case you believe was wrongly decided by a lower court. Focus on how you, as the appellant, would argue that the lower court's decision should be overturned. Identify the respondent's likely counterarguments.

By engaging with these exercises, you will deepen your understanding of the key roles in legal cases and develop the strategic thinking necessary to navigate the legal process effectively.

Chapter 4: Filing a Case: Understanding Pleadings

“"Pleadings are the foundation of a case. If the foundation is weak, the entire structure is in danger of collapsing."

- **Sir Edward Coke**

The Beginning of Every Legal Battle

Imagine standing on the brink of a monumental legal battle. It could be the case that changes a life, impacts a community, or shifts the very interpretation of the law. But before the courtroom is filled with arguments, rebuttals, and testimonies, there is a quieter, yet equally significant, moment, the filing of a **pleading**. This moment is not just procedural; it is the foundation upon which the entire case rests.

A pleading is the first voice of a case. It tells the court, “This is why we are here.” Every word in a complaint or petition has weight, for it sets the tone and defines the legal arguments that will follow. It draws the battlefield, identifying the issues that will be debated. Understanding pleadings is essential for every law student and lawyer because it is through this language that you give birth to your case.

In this chapter, we will explore the anatomy of pleadings, the types of documents involved in filing a case, and the importance of clarity and precision in drafting. With examples from significant cases that have shaped legal history, we will understand how pleadings have not only initiated legal processes but have shaped the trajectory of justice itself.

What is a Pleading? A Legal Foundation

A **pleading** is more than just a formal legal document; it is the core communication that initiates the legal process. In essence, a pleading tells the court what the legal issue is, what the facts are, and what relief the plaintiff seeks. Every pleading is a structured narrative, crafted with both legal precision and rhetorical power. It frames the case, allowing the court to focus on the specific matters at hand.

But a pleading is not just a complaint or a petition. It is also a reflection of the lawyer's understanding of the law. In a well-drafted pleading, the law comes alive. The skill of writing a pleading is to ensure that the facts and the law intertwine, creating a compelling story that captures the essence of the legal issue.

Case Study: Golak Nath v. State of Punjab (1967)

In the landmark case of **Golak Nath v. State of Punjab** (1967), the issue was whether Parliament had the power to amend fundamental rights under the Constitution of India. The petitioners, led by I.C. Golak Nath, filed a **writ petition** in the Supreme Court, arguing that Parliament could not amend the fundamental rights guaranteed under Part III of the Constitution. This petition laid the groundwork for the entire legal battle.

The pleadings in the Golak Nath case were crucial because they framed the legal question that would eventually lead to a historic ruling. The Supreme Court, in its judgment, held that Parliament did not have the power to amend fundamental rights, a decision that was later overturned by the basic structure doctrine in **Kesavananda Bharati v. State of Kerala** (1973). Yet, it was the precision and clarity of the pleadings in the Golak Nath case that brought the issue to the forefront of Indian constitutional law.

In this case, the pleading did not just tell a story; it framed a constitutional dilemma, forcing the court to confront the question of parliamentary supremacy versus fundamental rights. This is the power of a well-crafted pleading, it can force a legal system to reconsider its principles.

Types of Pleadings: The Legal Instruments of Communication

Understanding the different types of pleadings is essential for any legal practitioner. Each document serves a specific purpose, and knowing how to use them effectively can be the difference between a successful case and one that flounders.

Complaint and Petition: Setting the Stage

The **complaint** or **petition** is the first document filed in a legal case. It is the initial pleading that sets out the plaintiff's claims. It includes a statement of facts, the legal basis for the claim, and the relief sought by the plaintiff. This document is the foundation upon which the case is built.

In civil cases, the complaint is a tool for the plaintiff to lay out their grievances. In **P.A. Inamdar v. State of Maharashtra** (2005), a case concerning private educational institutions' rights to determine admission criteria, the petitioners filed a petition challenging government interference in their autonomy. The clarity and focus of the petition were crucial in persuading the Supreme Court to rule in favor of the petitioners. The pleadings focused on the violation of fundamental rights, effectively setting the stage for a landmark judgment that upheld the autonomy of private institutions.

In contrast, in criminal cases, the filing of a **charge sheet** (a form of pleading) by the police sets out the charges against the accused. In the famous **Arushi Talwar Murder Case** (2008), the charge sheet filed by the police became a highly debated document. Its weaknesses, omissions, and inconsistencies were criticized, highlighting how even in criminal cases, the quality of pleadings can have profound consequences.

Motion: Asking the Court for Immediate Action

A **motion** is a formal request to the court for a specific ruling or order. Motions are critical in both civil and criminal cases, as they can request a wide variety of actions, such as dismissing a case, compelling discovery, or granting summary judgment.

In the **Indra Sawhney v. Union of India** (1992) case, which dealt with reservations in government jobs, numerous motions were filed, including motions for interim relief. The sheer volume of motions in this case highlighted their strategic importance in shaping the course of legal proceedings. Through motions, the parties asked the court to issue temporary orders while the case was being heard, which had a significant impact on the interim reliefs granted during the litigation.

The lesson here is that a motion is not just a procedural step, it can be a powerful strategic tool. It can alter the course of a case long before a final decision is made.

Affidavit: Presenting Facts Under Oath

An **affidavit** is a written statement made under oath, used to present facts or evidence in support of a party's case. Affidavits are crucial because they allow parties to present their version of events to the court in a formal, legally binding document.

One of the most significant uses of affidavits in Indian history was in the **Narmada Bachao Andolan v. Union of India** (2000) case. The affidavits filed by the petitioners, including environmental activists, documented the environmental and social impacts of the Sardar Sarovar Dam project. These affidavits were instrumental in presenting evidence about the displacement of communities and the ecological damage caused by the project. The case, which was a clash between development and environmental protection, showcased how affidavits can present compelling narratives and factual accounts that the court may not otherwise be able to consider.

In this case, the affidavits were more than just formal documents, they were the voice of the voiceless, bringing to light the suffering of marginalized communities.

The Role of Clarity in Pleadings: Simplicity as a Strategy

It may be tempting to fill pleadings with legal jargon and complex language, but the most effective pleadings are often those that are clear and simple. Clarity ensures that the court understands the issues at hand and can focus on the legal principles involved. It is not enough to know the law; a lawyer must also communicate it effectively.

Case Study: Vishakha v. State of Rajasthan (1997)

In the case of **Vishakha v. State of Rajasthan** (1997), the petitioners sought to establish guidelines for preventing sexual harassment in the workplace. The pleadings were straightforward, focusing on the lack of statutory mechanisms to protect women at work. The clarity of the pleadings allowed the Supreme Court to focus on the core issue and issue the **Vishakha Guidelines**, which have since become the basis for workplace harassment laws in India.

This case illustrates how simplicity in pleading can lead to monumental legal change. The petitioners did not complicate their argument with unnecessary details. Instead, they focused on the essential question: What can the court do to fill the legal vacuum and protect the rights of working women?

The Art of Precision in Legal Writing

Precision in legal pleadings is not just about being concise, it's about ensuring that every word serves a purpose. In **Minerva Mills v. Union of India** (1980), the petitioners challenged the constitutional validity of amendments that sought to curtail judicial review. The pleadings were sharply focused on the interpretation of the basic structure doctrine. Because the arguments were presented with precision, the court was able to engage deeply with the issue and ultimately reinforce the doctrine of basic structure, holding that judicial review is an essential feature of the Indian Constitution.

In this case, precision was the key to success. By framing the issue clearly and concisely, the petitioners forced the court to confront the core legal principle without being distracted by peripheral issues.

The Discovery Process: Unveiling the Truth

Once pleadings have been filed, the legal process moves into the **discovery** phase. This is where the parties gather information to support their claims and defenses. Discovery includes several key elements, such as **interrogatories**, **depositions**, and **requests for production of documents**. The purpose of discovery is to ensure that both parties have access to all the relevant facts before the trial begins.

Interrogatories: Asking the Right Questions

Interrogatories are written questions that one party sends to the other, seeking information relevant to the case. The responses are given under oath and can be used as evidence during the trial. Interrogatories are a crucial tool for gathering facts, but they must be carefully crafted to avoid eliciting irrelevant or unhelpful information.

In the **Salman Khan Hit-and-Run Case** (2002), interrogatories were used extensively during the discovery phase to clarify the events leading up to the accident. The prosecution used interrogatories to question witnesses about their recollections of the night in question. These responses played a crucial role in establishing the timeline of events, which eventually contributed to the conviction of Salman Khan in the initial trial (though later acquitted by the High Court). The case highlights how interrogatories can bring clarity to the factual disputes in a case.

Depositions: The Testimony Before the Trial

A **deposition** is an out-of-court testimony given under oath, often recorded for later use during the trial. Depositions allow both parties to question witnesses and gather testimony that can be used to challenge the credibility of witnesses or supplement the facts presented at trial.

In the **OJ Simpson Trial** (1995), depositions played a key role in the civil trial that followed the criminal acquittal. The depositions of several key witnesses, including law enforcement officers and forensic experts, were critical in building the case against Simpson in the civil suit, where he was found liable for wrongful death. The depositions exposed inconsistencies in testimonies and provided a foundation for the jury's eventual finding against Simpson.

Depositions, therefore, are a powerful discovery tool because they allow attorneys to lock in testimony before the trial begins. In doing so, they can anticipate the arguments and strategies of the opposing side, giving them an advantage in court.

Challenges in Pleadings: When Precision Meets Complexity

While clarity and precision are essential, pleadings often face unique challenges in cases involving multiple parties, complex legal issues, or conflicting facts. When drafting pleadings, a lawyer must strike a balance between simplicity and the need to present a comprehensive legal argument.

Case Study: Ram Jethmalani's Defense in Harshad Mehta Scam

In the **Harshad Mehta Securities Scam** (1992), one of the largest financial scandals in India, Ram Jethmalani represented the interests of Mehta, who was accused of manipulating stock prices and siphoning funds from banks. The complexity of the case, which involved numerous parties, thousands of transactions, and multiple legal jurisdictions, made the drafting of pleadings an immense challenge.

Jethmalani's defense relied on meticulous pleadings that broke down the complex financial transactions into understandable legal arguments. The pleadings focused on the technicalities of financial regulations and securities law, challenging the prosecution's narrative of criminal conspiracy. While Mehta was eventually convicted, the pleadings in this case showcased the strategic importance of addressing complexity with clarity, ensuring that even the most complicated cases are presented coherently.

Real-Life Consequences: When Pleadings Fail

It is equally important to recognize the consequences of poorly drafted pleadings. When pleadings are vague, incomplete, or imprecise, they can undermine a case even before it reaches trial.

The Bhopal Gas Tragedy Case (1984)

In the **Union Carbide Corporation v. Union of India** (1989), also known as the Bhopal Gas Tragedy case, one of the critical failures was the inadequacy of the initial pleadings filed by the Indian government. The complaint did not fully capture the scale of the disaster, nor did it adequately outline the legal grounds for holding Union Carbide responsible for the gas leak that killed thousands of people.

This failure in the pleadings was one reason why Union Carbide was able to negotiate a much lower settlement than initially anticipated, $470 million, an amount widely criticized as insufficient given the magnitude of the tragedy. This case underscores the importance of strong pleadings in establishing the gravity of a case and securing adequate relief.

Exercises in Drafting Pleadings

Understanding the theory of pleadings is essential, but applying that knowledge is the key to becoming a skilled lawyer. Below are some practical exercises to help you refine your ability to draft effective pleadings.

Exercise 1: Drafting a Complaint

Given the following facts, draft a complaint for a civil case:

- A tenant is suing their landlord for failing to repair a leaking roof, despite multiple requests.

- The tenant claims that the landlord's negligence has caused damage to their property and made the premises uninhabitable.

- The tenant seeks damages and a court order compelling the landlord to make the necessary repairs.

Your task is to draft the complaint, clearly stating the facts, the legal grounds for the claim, and the relief sought.

Exercise 2:
Writing a Motion for Summary Judgment

In a hypothetical defamation case, the defendant is asking the court to dismiss the case based on the lack of evidence. Draft a motion for summary judgment, arguing that the plaintiff has failed to meet the burden of proof.

Exercise 3:
Responding to Interrogatories

Imagine you are representing a client in a breach of contract case. You have received interrogatories from the opposing counsel asking for details about the timeline of events leading up to the breach. Draft your responses, ensuring that you provide sufficient information without revealing unnecessary details that could harm your client's position.

Filing a case begins with a pleading, but a pleading is much more than a formality, it is the foundation upon which your case is built. As you move forward in your legal career, remember that the clarity, precision, and strategy with which you draft your pleadings will often determine the success or failure of your case.

Each word in a pleading is a thread in the fabric of justice. Each document filed is a step closer to a resolution. And with each case, no matter how small or large, the pleading is your first opportunity to tell the court, "This is why we are here."

"The law is reason, free from passion, but the practice of law begins with the passion of a well-crafted argument."

\- **Aristotle**

Chapter 5: Trial Terminology

"The trial is the crucible in which the truth is tested. Every word, every piece of evidence, every argument is weighed and measured against the standard of justice"

- **Justice Oliver Wendell Holmes Jr.**

The Symphony of the Courtroom

Imagine standing at the edge of a battlefield, a quiet yet intense anticipation fills the air. The courtroom is such a battlefield, and at the center of this arena is the trial, a space where the truth is sought, where arguments are sharpened, and where justice either ascends or stumbles. But the trial is not a chaotic clash; it is an orchestrated symphony, a precise dance of procedures and terminology that you, as a lawyer, must master.

Every word spoken, every motion filed, every objection raised is part of a legal language that, when wielded correctly, has the power to turn the tide in favor of your client. To navigate the trial stage effectively, you must understand the key terminology that defines its various phases. From the opening statement that frames the narrative to the verdict that delivers justice, each term is a building block, creating the foundation for a fair trial.

In this chapter, we will break down the essential terminology used in trials. Using real-world examples, precedents, and case studies, we will explore how these terms are not just legal jargon but vital tools that shape the course of justice. As you delve into each section, you will see how the mastery of trial terminology is not just about knowing the words, it is about understanding their power and purpose.

Opening Statement: Setting the Stage

The **opening statement** is where the trial truly begins. It is the lawyer's first opportunity to address the court and the jury, to frame the story that will unfold during the trial. The purpose of the opening statement is to give a roadmap of the case, presenting the facts and the expected evidence without argument or persuasion.

Crafting the Narrative

The opening statement is not the time for legal arguments; it is about telling a story that connects with the jury on a human level. A well-crafted opening statement gives the jury a clear picture of the events, making them emotionally invested in the outcome.

Consider the **O.J. Simpson trial** (1995), one of the most famous criminal trials in history. The opening statements made by both the prosecution and defense were crucial in shaping the narrative. The prosecution, led by Marcia Clark, framed Simpson as a violent man who murdered his ex-wife and her friend. On the other hand, the defense, led by Johnnie Cochran, focused on police misconduct and racial bias, setting the stage for the argument that Simpson had been framed.

The power of an opening statement lies in its ability to set expectations and create a narrative lens through which the jury views the evidence. In the O.J. Simpson case, the defense's narrative of systemic racism and police corruption resonated strongly with the jury, contributing to the eventual acquittal.

Case Study: Aarushi Talwar Murder Case (India)

In India, the **Aarushi Talwar murder case** (2008) similarly hinged on the narrative presented during the trial. The prosecution's opening statement painted the Talwars as controlling parents who murdered their daughter out of rage. The defense, however, argued that the investigation was riddled with incompetence and manipulation. Each side's opening statement set the stage for how the jury would interpret the evidence, and ultimately, the verdict rested heavily on the framing of the facts.

Practical Tip: Your opening statement should be clear, concise, and emotionally resonant. Remember that the jury will interpret the rest of the trial through the lens you provide. Use simple language, avoid legal jargon, and focus on building a connection with the jury.

Examination and Cross-Examination: Unveiling the Truth

Once the opening statements are made, the heart of the trial begins with the presentation of evidence through **examination** and **cross-examination**. This is where witnesses are called, facts are established, and the credibility of evidence is tested.

Direct Examination: Telling the Client's Story

Direct examination occurs when a lawyer questions their own witnesses to establish facts that support their case. The questions must be open-ended, allowing the witness to provide a narrative without leading them to specific answers.

In the **K.M. Nanavati v. State of Maharashtra** (1961) case, which became one of India's most sensational trials, the direct examination of Sylvia Nanavati, the wife of the accused, was pivotal. Her testimony regarding her affair with Prem Ahuja and the events leading to the murder shaped the entire case. During direct examination, the defense carefully presented Sylvia's version of events to humanize the accused and portray him as a man driven by sudden and grave provocation.

Direct examination is where the foundation of your case is laid. You bring forward facts, one by one, building a story that aligns with your client's version of events.

Cross-Examination: Challenging the Opponent's Evidence

Cross-examination is perhaps the most powerful tool in a lawyer's arsenal. It is where you get to challenge the credibility of the opposing party's witnesses. Unlike direct examination, cross-examination questions are leading, designed to elicit "yes" or "no" answers and expose inconsistencies in the witness's testimony.

In the **Jessica Lal murder case** (2006), cross-examination was a critical element in uncovering the contradictions in the defense's narrative. The case involved the high-profile murder of a model, Jessica Lal, and the cross-examination of key witnesses exposed significant discrepancies in their statements. The cross-examination effectively dismantled the defense's attempt to obscure the facts, leading to the conviction of Manu Sharma.

In cross-examination, your goal is to control the witness's testimony and weaken the opposing party's case. It is not about asking open-ended questions but about leading the witness to admit facts that support your case or undermine their credibility.

Case Study: Brown v. Board of Education (USA)

In **Brown v. Board of Education** (1954), a landmark U.S. Supreme Court case that challenged racial segregation in public schools, cross-examination played a crucial role. The plaintiffs' attorneys used cross-examination to challenge the expert testimony that supported segregation, highlighting the flawed reasoning behind "separate but equal." The case ultimately led to a ruling that segregation was unconstitutional, demonstrating the transformative power of effective cross-examination.

Practical Tip: During cross-examination, maintain control of the witness by asking concise, targeted questions. Avoid giving the witness room to explain or justify their answers. Your goal is to extract damaging admissions or inconsistencies, so be precise and purposeful.

Objections: Protecting the Integrity of the Trial

Throughout a trial, lawyers may raise **objections** to challenge the admissibility of evidence or the line of questioning. Objections are an essential part of maintaining the fairness of the trial and ensuring that the jury only hears evidence that is legally relevant.

Common Objections and Their Purpose

Some of the most common objections include:

- **Hearsay**: Statements made outside of court that are offered as evidence of the truth of the matter asserted. For example, if a witness testifies, "I heard him say he was guilty," this is typically inadmissible as hearsay.

- **Relevance**: Evidence must be directly related to the case. If the opposing counsel introduces facts that do not have any bearing on the case, you can object on the grounds of relevance.

- **Leading Questions**: In direct examination, leading questions (those that suggest the answer) are generally not allowed.

In the **K.M. Nanavati v. State of Maharashtra** case, multiple objections were raised during the trial, particularly regarding the admissibility of certain pieces of evidence. The defense objected to the inclusion of Sylvia's letters, arguing they were irrelevant to the case. Objections like these, when successful, can prevent damaging evidence from being admitted.

Case Study: The Trial of Oscar Pistorius (South Africa)

During the trial of South African athlete **Oscar Pistorius** for the murder of his girlfriend Reeva Steenkamp, objections were frequently raised concerning the admission of forensic evidence. The defense objected to the admissibility of certain ballistic reports, arguing that they were speculative and not grounded in fact. These objections were crucial in shaping the evidence that was ultimately presented to the jury, highlighting how objections can significantly impact the outcome of a trial.

Practical Tip: When raising an objection, be clear and concise. Cite the specific rule or legal principle that supports your objection. Objecting not only protects your case from prejudicial evidence but also forces the court to stay within the boundaries of the law.

The Verdict: The Final Judgment

After the presentation of evidence, examination, cross-examination, and closing arguments, the fate of the case rests in the hands of the **verdict**. The verdict is the formal decision made by the judge (in a bench trial) or the jury (in a jury trial) regarding the guilt or innocence of the defendant in criminal cases, or the liability of the defendant in civil cases.

The Process of Deliberation

In cases involving a jury, after closing arguments, the jury retires to deliberate on the evidence presented during the trial. The deliberation process involves discussing the facts, reviewing evidence, and applying the law as instructed by the judge. The jury must reach a unanimous decision in most criminal cases, while in civil cases, a majority may suffice depending on the jurisdiction.

In the **Nirbhaya Rape Case** (2012), the verdict was delivered after an intense trial that captured the attention of the entire nation. The jury in this case was replaced by the judge's final ruling (as is common in Indian criminal cases), and the defendants were found guilty of rape and murder. The verdict was a culmination of public outcry and a meticulous presentation of evidence, demonstrating how the trial process, when conducted effectively, can lead to justice.

Case Study: The Trial of Adolf Eichmann (Israel)

In the post-World War II **trial of Adolf Eichmann** (1961), one of the architects of the Holocaust, the verdict represented a significant moment in international law. Eichmann was tried in Israel for crimes against humanity, and the verdict found him guilty on multiple counts. The trial was notable not only for its historical significance but also for the legal procedures involved. The verdict was the final affirmation of Eichmann's responsibility for one of the darkest chapters in human history, demonstrating the profound impact a verdict can have in delivering justice and closure.

Practical Tip: The verdict is the culmination of your work in the trial. While you cannot control the outcome, you can influence it by presenting clear, compelling evidence, and persuasive arguments. Every aspect of the trial, from the opening statement to the final objection, contributes to the verdict.

Jury Instructions: Guiding the Path to Justice

Before the jury begins its deliberation, the judge provides **jury instructions**, which are the legal standards the jury must use to decide the case. These instructions outline the elements of the offense (in criminal cases) or the legal requirements for liability (in civil cases) and explain the burden of proof.

The Importance of Clear Jury Instructions

Clear and accurate jury instructions are critical because they ensure that the jury applies the law correctly. If jury instructions are vague or incomplete, it can lead to an incorrect verdict or provide grounds for an appeal.

In **R v. Ratten** (1972), a UK case that dealt with the admissibility of evidence and the role of intent in criminal liability, the clarity of jury instructions was a key issue. The court had to ensure that the jury understood the legal distinctions between manslaughter and murder. This case highlights how crucial jury instructions are in guiding the jury to a legally sound verdict.

Practical Tip: As a lawyer, you can request specific jury instructions that favor your client's position. Work closely with the judge to ensure that the jury is given clear, fair, and accurate guidance.

The Role of Evidence: Building the Case

At the heart of every trial is the presentation of **evidence**. Evidence can take many forms, including witness testimony, documents, forensic reports, and physical objects. The rules governing the admissibility and relevance of evidence are critical in determining what the jury or judge will consider when making their decision.

Admissibility of Evidence

Not all evidence is admissible in court. For evidence to be admissible, it must be relevant to the case and must comply with rules governing its form, such as the **hearsay rule**, which excludes certain out-of-court statements, and the **best evidence rule**, which requires that the original document be produced in court unless a valid exception applies.

In **State v. Afzal Guru** (2005), the trial involving the 2001 Indian Parliament attack, the admissibility of evidence was hotly contested. The defense objected to the admission of certain confessions and documents, arguing that they were obtained under duress. The court ultimately admitted some of this evidence, but the controversy surrounding its admissibility became a significant issue in the public's perception of the trial's fairness.

Chain of Custody

In criminal cases, maintaining the **chain of custody** is essential for ensuring that evidence has not been tampered with or altered. The chain of custody refers to the documentation that tracks the movement and handling of physical evidence from the time it is collected until it is presented in court.

In the **Arushi Talwar Murder Case**, questions about the chain of custody of forensic evidence, such as blood samples and DNA, undermined the credibility of the evidence presented at trial. The defense argued that the mishandling of evidence had compromised the investigation, leading to an acquittal in the High Court after the initial conviction.

Practical Tip: Ensure that all evidence you plan to introduce at trial is properly authenticated and meets the legal requirements for admissibility. Be prepared to challenge the admissibility of any evidence that does not meet these standards.

The Closing Argument: The Final Word

The **closing argument** is your last opportunity to address the jury or judge. It is where you tie together the evidence, reinforce your legal arguments, and make an emotional appeal for justice.

Persuasion and Precision

A powerful closing argument weaves together the facts, the law, and the emotional elements of the case. It should not introduce new evidence but rather synthesize the information presented during the trial into a cohesive narrative.

In the **Nirbhaya Rape Case** (2012), the prosecution's closing argument focused on the brutality of the crime and the overwhelming evidence against the accused. The defense, on the other hand, tried to raise doubts about the integrity of the investigation. The prosecution's ability to succinctly summarize the evidence and appeal to the jury's sense of justice played a significant role in securing the conviction.

Case Study: Nelson Mandela's Rivonia Trial (1964)

In **Nelson Mandela's Rivonia Trial**, his closing statement was not just a defense but a powerful declaration of his fight against apartheid. Mandela famously stated, "I have cherished the ideal of a democratic and free society in which all persons live together in harmony and with equal opportunities. It is an ideal for which I am prepared to die." His words resonated far beyond the courtroom, shaping not only the trial's outcome but the course of South African history.

Practical Tip: In your closing argument, aim to create a lasting impression. Summarize the evidence clearly, refute the opposing side's claims, and make an emotional appeal that resonates with the jury or judge.

Conclusion: Mastering the Trial Process

The trial is where the law comes alive. It is the culmination of preparation, strategy, and understanding of key legal principles and terminology. Each stage of the trial, from the opening statement to the verdict, requires a lawyer to be both a storyteller and a tactician. The words you choose, the objections you raise, and the evidence you present all contribute to the final outcome.

Understanding trial terminology is not just about learning the right words; it is about mastering the process that those words represent. It is about knowing when to object, when to push harder on cross-examination, and when to step back and let the evidence speak for itself.

"In the end, a trial is a reflection of society's pursuit of truth. And truth, when brought to light through the right words, can be the most powerful tool of all."

\- **Nani Palkhivala**

Exercises and Practical Applications

1. **Draft an Opening Statement**:

Imagine you are representing a client in a personal injury case. Draft an opening statement that frames the facts of the case in a compelling narrative for the jury.

2. **Prepare for Cross-Examination**:

Review a witness's deposition in a hypothetical breach of contract case. Prepare five cross-examination questions designed to expose inconsistencies in the witness's testimony.

3. **Raise an Objection**:

In a mock trial scenario, the opposing counsel presents hearsay evidence. Write out your objection, citing the relevant rule of evidence and explaining why the testimony should be excluded.

4. **Develop a Closing Argument**:

Based on a criminal case involving theft, draft a closing argument that summarizes the evidence and persuades the jury to deliver a verdict in your client's favor.

By engaging with these exercises, you will deepen your understanding of trial terminology and sharpen your skills in the art of courtroom advocacy.

Chapter 6: Judgment and Appeals

"The ultimate aim of the law is to secure justice, and a judgment, to be just, must be based on a sound understanding of the facts and the law."

\- **Justice Benjamin N. Cardozo**

The Finality That Is Never Final

Imagine standing in a courtroom, the air thick with anticipation as the judge prepares to deliver the judgment. It is a moment that feels final, conclusive, as if justice is about to take a definitive shape. But the truth is, a judgment is rarely the end of the story. It is a decision, yes, but it is not necessarily the final word. The beauty of the law is that it allows for dissent, for a challenge, for the pursuit of further clarity. And so, from every judgment, an appeal may arise, a second chance to reshape the outcome, to challenge the interpretation, to argue once again for what is right.

The trial may have ended, but the journey to justice continues. In this chapter, we will explore the intricate world of **judgments and appeals**. We will unravel the anatomy of a judgment, examine how courts reach their decisions, and explore the essential terminology involved in this process. Furthermore, we will delve into the realm of **appeals**, the procedural path that gives litigants an opportunity to challenge judgments in higher courts. Through case law and real-life examples, you will understand how judgments and appeals are the twin pillars that support the structure of legal practice.

Let us begin by asking ourselves: What truly happens when a judgment is delivered? How does the law transform through the process of appeal? This chapter is about understanding that, in the legal world, every conclusion is also a potential new beginning.

Judgment: The Decision at the End of a Trial

A **judgment** is the official decision made by a judge or jury at the conclusion of a trial. It is the declaration of the court regarding the rights and liabilities of the parties involved. The judgment could be in favor of the plaintiff or the defendant, and it could also come with remedies such as damages, injunctions, or declaratory relief.

Anatomy of a Judgment

A judgment consists of several key components that outline the reasoning and legal principles on which the court's decision is based. These components include:

- **Findings of Fact**: The judge or jury's determination of the factual issues presented in the case. These facts form the foundation upon which the legal reasoning is built.

- **Conclusions of Law**: The application of legal principles to the facts of the case. This section outlines the court's interpretation of the law and how it applies to the issues at hand.

- **Relief or Remedy**: The formal declaration of the judgment, which could include monetary damages, orders for specific performance, or other remedies such as an injunction.

In the case of **Vishaka v. State of Rajasthan** (1997), the judgment was groundbreaking not just for its ruling, but for the clarity with which the court outlined the need for guidelines to prevent sexual harassment in the workplace. The judgment did more than resolve the dispute; it laid the groundwork for future legal protection of women in India. The Supreme Court issued a set of guidelines, known as the **Vishaka Guidelines**, which remained in place until the enactment of formal legislation in 2013.

The structure of the judgment in **Vishaka** became a template for future cases involving the interpretation of constitutional protections and human rights. The court's conclusions of law in this case set a powerful precedent, illustrating how judgments do more than just settle disputes, they shape the future of legal practice.

The Power of Precedent in Judgments

In common law systems, judgments create **precedents**. A precedent is a judicial decision that serves as an authoritative example for future cases involving similar facts or issues of law. The doctrine of **stare decisis**, meaning "to stand by things decided," requires courts to follow established precedents to maintain consistency and predictability in the law.

The landmark case of **Donoghue v. Stevenson** (1932) is often cited as the foundation of modern tort law and the duty of care. In this case, the judgment delivered by the House of Lords established the "neighbor principle," which holds that individuals must take reasonable care to avoid acts or omissions that could foreseeably cause harm to their "neighbors" (those who are closely and directly affected by their actions).

This case illustrates how a judgment can go beyond the resolution of a particular dispute and serve as a cornerstone for an entire body of law. The principle established in **Donoghue v. Stevenson** has been applied and expanded upon in countless cases since, becoming a fundamental concept in negligence law around the world.

Judgments, therefore, are not just the final word on a specific case, they become part of the living body of law, influencing future legal decisions and shaping societal norms.

Types of Judgments: Understanding the Legal Outcomes

While all judgments serve the purpose of resolving disputes, there are different types of judgments based on the nature of the case and the stage at which the judgment is rendered. Understanding these types is crucial for any lawyer, as each has different implications for the parties involved.

Judgment on the Merits

A **judgment on the merits** is a decision made after the court has heard the facts of the case and has applied the law to those facts. It reflects a full and complete resolution of the legal issues presented, and it often involves a determination of the parties' rights and liabilities.

In **Olga Tellis v. Bombay Municipal Corporation** (1985), the Supreme Court of India delivered a judgment on the merits regarding the rights of slum dwellers who were being evicted from their homes in Mumbai. The court ruled that the right to life under Article 21 of the Constitution included the right to livelihood, and therefore, the state could not evict people from their homes without providing alternative shelter or opportunities.

This judgment was significant not only because it ruled in favor of the petitioners but also because it expanded the interpretation of Article 21 to include the right to livelihood. The judgment on the merits in **Olga Tellis** continues to influence housing rights and state policies in India.

Default Judgment

A **default judgment** occurs when one party fails to appear in court or respond to the legal claims made against them. In such cases, the court may issue a judgment in favor of the party that has appeared, based on the facts presented.

A notable case where a default judgment played a significant role is **Anil Kumble v. Jemson Antao** (1999). Indian cricketer Anil Kumble filed a defamation suit against Jemson Antao, who had allegedly made false and damaging statements about him. Antao failed to appear in court, leading to a default judgment in favor of Kumble. The court awarded substantial damages to Kumble, reinforcing the importance of appearing in court and defending one's case.

Default judgments serve as a reminder that the legal process must be respected, and parties who fail to respond risk losing their case without even having the opportunity to present their defense.

Summary Judgment

A **summary judgment** is granted when there is no genuine dispute of material fact, and the moving party is entitled to judgment as a matter of law. Summary judgments are typically issued when the facts of the case are undisputed, and the only issue before the court is the application of the law.

In **Swami Motors v. Ashok Leyland Ltd.** (1997), a dispute arose over a breach of contract in the supply of commercial vehicles. The defendant, Ashok Leyland, moved for summary judgment, arguing that the facts of the case were not in dispute and that they were entitled to judgment based on the terms of the contract. The court agreed, issuing a summary judgment in favor of the defendant, effectively resolving the case without a full trial.

Summary judgments are often sought in cases where one party believes that the other has no valid legal defense and that further proceedings would be unnecessary. While it saves time and resources, summary judgment requires a thorough understanding of both the facts and the law to be successfully argued.

Appeals: The Path to Challenging a Judgment

A judgment is not always the final word in a legal dispute. The losing party often has the right to appeal the decision to a higher court, seeking a reversal or modification of the judgment. Appeals are an integral part of the legal process, allowing for the correction of errors and the refinement of legal principles.

The Right to Appeal: A Safeguard of Justice

The **right to appeal** is a fundamental safeguard in any legal system. It ensures that parties have a second opportunity to argue their case before a higher authority and that potential errors made by the lower court can be rectified. Appeals can be based on various grounds, including errors of law, errors of fact, or procedural irregularities.

In **Maneka Gandhi v. Union of India** (1978), after the government's decision to impound her passport, Maneka Gandhi exercised her right to appeal the government's action. The Supreme Court of India ruled in her favor, significantly expanding the scope of Article 21 (the right to life and personal liberty) and ensuring that the government could not act arbitrarily in restricting personal freedoms. This appeal not only protected Gandhi's individual rights but also established a broader legal precedent regarding the protection of personal liberty.

The right to appeal is thus more than just a second chance for the litigants, it is a mechanism for ensuring that the legal system remains fair, just, and accountable.

The Grounds for Appeal

There are several common grounds upon which

an appeal may be based:

- **Error of Law**: When the lower court has incorrectly interpreted or applied the law.

- **Error of Fact**: When the findings of fact by the lower court are clearly erroneous.

- **Procedural Irregularities**: When there have been violations of the procedural rules that affect the fairness of the trial.

A landmark case that highlights the importance of appealing on legal grounds is **Roe v. Wade** (1973), in the United States. The appeal in this case challenged the constitutionality of state laws that restricted access to abortion. The U.S. Supreme Court's ruling in favor of **Roe** fundamentally altered reproductive rights in the country. The appeal was based on constitutional grounds, particularly the right to privacy, and the judgment that followed became one of the most significant rulings in U.S. legal history.

Grounds for appeal often reflect not just the errors of the lower court but the evolving interpretations of the law itself. Successful appeals can lead to landmark judgments that reshape legal doctrines, as seen in **Roe v. Wade**.

The Appeals Process: From Filing to Judgment

The appeals process is more than just rearguing the case in a higher court. It follows a structured procedural path, from filing a notice of appeal to presenting oral arguments before the appellate judges.

Notice of Appeal: The First Step

The first formal step in the appeals process is the filing of a **notice of appeal**. This document informs the lower court and the opposing party that the appellant intends to challenge the judgment. The notice must be filed within a specific timeframe, known as the **appeal period**, which varies depending on the jurisdiction and the type of case.

In the **Suresh Kumar Koushal v. Naz Foundation** (2013) case, which dealt with the constitutionality of Section 377 of the Indian Penal Code (criminalizing homosexual acts), the judgment of the Delhi High Court was appealed to the Supreme Court. The appeal challenged the lower court's decision to decriminalize homosexual acts, and the Supreme Court ultimately reinstated Section 377. This decision was later reversed in **Navtej Singh Johar v. Union of India** (2018), after further appeals and legal arguments.

The filing of the notice of appeal in **Naz Foundation** marked the beginning of a protracted legal battle that eventually led to the decriminalization of homosexuality in India, a testament to the evolving nature of legal interpretations through the appeals process.

Briefs: The Written Arguments

Once the notice of appeal is filed, both parties submit written arguments, known as **briefs**, to the appellate court. The appellant's brief outlines the legal errors made by the lower court and argues for the judgment to be reversed or modified. The appellee's brief defends the lower court's ruling and explains why the judgment should be upheld.

In **Miranda v. Arizona** (1966), the U.S. Supreme Court's decision hinged on the legal briefs submitted by both sides. The appellant, Ernesto Miranda, argued that his confession should not have been admissible in court because he had not been informed of his rights to remain silent and have an attorney present. The

Miranda Rights, as they are now known, became a fundamental part of American criminal procedure, ensuring that individuals are aware of their rights when in police custody.

The quality of the written briefs in an appeal is critical. A well-crafted brief can persuade the appellate judges to view the case through a different lens, even before oral arguments are made.

Oral Arguments: Presenting the Case in Court

After the submission of briefs, the appellate court may hold **oral arguments**, where the lawyers for both sides present their cases before the judges. Unlike trial court, where facts are established, appellate oral arguments focus primarily on the interpretation of the law. Lawyers must be prepared to answer pointed questions from the judges and clarify any ambiguities in the written briefs.

In **Brown v. Board of Education** (1954), the oral arguments before the U.S. Supreme Court were pivotal in persuading the justices to overturn the doctrine of "separate but equal." Thurgood Marshall, representing the plaintiffs, argued that racial segregation in public schools violated the Equal Protection Clause of the Fourteenth Amendment. The oral arguments allowed the justices to probe deeper into the constitutional questions at hand, leading to a unanimous decision that reshaped American society.

Oral arguments in an appeal require precision, clarity, and the ability to respond to judicial inquiries in real time. They offer an opportunity to reinforce the points made in the written briefs and address any concerns the judges may have.

Appellate Court's Decision: Affirm, Reverse, or Remand

At the conclusion of the appeals process, the appellate court will issue its **decision**, which can take several forms:

- **Affirm**: The appellate court may **affirm** the lower court's judgment, meaning it agrees with the decision and upholds it in its entirety.

- **Reverse**: The appellate court may **reverse** the judgment, meaning it disagrees with the lower court's decision and overturns it.

- **Remand**: The appellate court may **remand** the case, meaning it sends the case back to the lower court for further proceedings, often with instructions for how to correct specific legal errors.

In **State of Tamil Nadu v. K. Balu** (2017), the Supreme Court of India initially banned the sale of alcohol within 500 meters of national and state highways to reduce road accidents. However, after further legal challenges, the court remanded the case back to the High Courts for re-evaluation, allowing for certain exceptions to the rule. The remand demonstrated how appellate courts can provide guidance without making a final determination, allowing lower courts to reexamine the facts under new legal standards.

Remanding a case often provides an opportunity for a more thorough examination of issues that were not fully addressed in the original trial, making it a critical component of the appellate process.

The Impact of Appeals: Shaping Legal Doctrine

Appeals are not just a tool for correcting errors; they play a fundamental role in shaping legal doctrine and evolving the law. Through the process of appeals, courts have the opportunity to reinterpret legal principles, resolve conflicting interpretations, and adapt the law to meet the changing needs of society.

Case Study: Kesavananda Bharati v. State of Kerala (1973)

One of the most significant appeals in Indian constitutional history is **Kesavananda Bharati v. State of Kerala** (1973). In this case, the petitioner, Kesavananda Bharati, challenged the validity of constitutional amendments that sought to limit judicial review and erode fundamental rights. The appeal was heard by a 13-judge bench of the Supreme Court, which delivered the landmark judgment establishing the **Basic Structure Doctrine**.

The court ruled that while Parliament has the power to amend the Constitution, it cannot alter the **basic structure** of the Constitution. This doctrine has since become a cornerstone of Indian constitutional law, ensuring that certain fundamental principles, such as the rule of law, separation of powers, and judicial review, remain inviolable.

The **Kesavananda Bharati** judgment was the result of an appeal, highlighting how appellate courts can play a transformative role in safeguarding constitutional values and preventing the overreach of legislative power.

Conclusion: The Journey Toward Justice

A judgment is not the end of a legal journey, it is a moment of reflection, a point from which new paths may emerge. Whether a party seeks to appeal or accepts the judgment as final, the legal process continues to evolve. The appellate system is a critical safeguard, ensuring that errors can be corrected, injustices rectified, and the law refined.

Each judgment, each appeal, brings us closer to the truth. And in the pursuit of justice, it is often in the act of challenging, questioning, and appealing that the law finds its most profound clarity.

"The final test of justice is not in the judgment delivered, but in the willingness to seek it again, in the hope that truth will prevail."

- **Justice H.R. Khanna**

Exercises and Practical Applications

1. Draft an Appellate Brief:

Imagine you are representing a client who lost a civil case in the trial court. Draft an appellate brief arguing that the trial court made an error of law in its interpretation of the contract. Use persuasive language to convince the appellate court to reverse the lower court's decision.

2. Analyze a Judgment:

Choose a recent Supreme Court judgment and break down its structure into findings of fact, conclusions of law, and relief or remedy. Discuss how the court's legal reasoning influenced the outcome of the case.

3. Prepare for Oral Arguments:

In a hypothetical criminal case where the defendant has been convicted of fraud, prepare oral arguments for an appeal. Focus on procedural errors during the trial that violated the defendant's right to a fair trial.

By engaging with these exercises, you will deepen your understanding of the appeals process and enhance your ability to navigate the complexities of judgments and appellate law.

Chapter 7: Constitutional Law Vocabulary

"A constitution is not meant to facilitate governance but to limit it. It is a charter of power, but also a charter of restrictions."

\- **Chief Justice John Marshall**

The Language of Constitutional Vision

What does it mean to speak the language of a Constitution? It is not merely about reading the words of the law; it is about engaging with the ideals that those words seek to protect. Constitutional law is the bedrock upon which nations are built, and the vocabulary of constitutional law is the key to unlocking its meaning. Every term, whether **sovereignty**, **due process**, or **federalism**, carries with it centuries of history, struggle, and evolution.

Understanding constitutional law begins with understanding its language. The words are not empty; they hold the hopes and dreams of societies, the tensions of conflicts, and the wisdom of resolutions. They are the foundation of rights, the boundaries of government power, and the reflection of collective identity. In this chapter, we will walk through the critical vocabulary of constitutional law, using real-world examples and case studies to illustrate how these words shape the destiny of nations.

Sovereignty:
The Foundation of Constitutional Power

At the heart of any constitutional system lies the concept of **sovereignty**. Sovereignty refers to the ultimate authority within a political entity, the power to make laws, enforce them, and ensure that no other authority supersedes this power within a certain territory. In constitutional law, sovereignty is often discussed in the context of whether it lies with the people, the state, or a monarch.

Case Study: The Indian Constitution and Popular Sovereignty

The **Constitution of India** embodies the principle of popular sovereignty, where the ultimate authority resides with the people. This is explicitly stated in the **Preamble** with the words "We, the people of India." The shift from colonial rule to independence was not merely a political transition but a transfer of sovereignty from the British Crown to the Indian people.

In the case of **S.R. Bommai v. Union of India** (1994), the Supreme Court of India was called upon to decide the limits of state sovereignty under the Indian Constitution. The central issue was whether the dismissal of state governments under **Article 356** of the Constitution (President's Rule) was constitutionally valid. The court held that state sovereignty is subordinate to the sovereignty of the Constitution itself, and the power of the President to dismiss a state government is not absolute but subject to judicial review. This ruling reinforced the idea that while states have autonomous powers, their sovereignty is derived from and limited by the Constitution, which represents the collective will of the people.

Federalism and Sovereignty: A Balancing Act

Sovereignty becomes even more complex in federal systems, where authority is divided between national and state governments. In the United States, for example, the **Tenth Amendment** reserves powers not delegated to the federal government to the states or the people, reflecting a balance between national and state sovereignty. This tension is often at the center of constitutional disputes, as seen in cases like **McCulloch v. Maryland** (1819), where the U.S.

Supreme Court ruled that federal law supersedes state law when the two conflict, reinforcing the supremacy of the national government in certain areas.

Separation of Powers: Dividing Authority to Prevent Tyranny

The concept of **separation of powers** refers to the division of government responsibilities into distinct branches, typically the executive, legislative, and judicial, to prevent any one branch from gaining too much power. This doctrine is a cornerstone of constitutional law, as it ensures that power is not concentrated in a single entity, which could lead to authoritarianism.

Montesquieu's Influence and Constitutional Practice

The idea of separation of powers can be traced back to **Montesquieu**, whose work ***The Spirit of the Laws*** inspired many modern constitutional frameworks, including the U.S. and Indian Constitutions. Montesquieu argued that the concentration of powers in a single authority could lead to despotism, and therefore, each branch of government must be independent and capable of checking the others.

In **Indira Gandhi v. Raj Narain** (1975), the concept of separation of powers was tested in India when the Prime Minister's election was challenged, leading to a declaration of emergency powers. The Supreme Court's ruling, which initially supported the expansion of executive power during the Emergency, was later seen as a misstep in protecting the separation of powers. In this period, the judiciary appeared to defer excessively to the executive branch, leading to a temporary erosion of checks and balances. This case highlighted the delicate nature of maintaining the separation of powers, particularly during times of political crisis.

Checks and Balances: Ensuring Accountability

The principle of **checks and balances** is a natural extension of the separation of powers. Each branch of government has the ability to limit the powers of the others, ensuring that no branch operates without oversight. This interplay of powers is crucial to maintaining a healthy democracy.

A notable example of this can be seen in the **Watergate Scandal** in the United States, where the judicial branch played a key role in limiting executive overreach. In **United States v. Nixon** (1974), the U.S. Supreme Court unanimously ruled that President Nixon had to release tape recordings of conversations related to the Watergate scandal, despite his claims of executive privilege. This case reaffirmed the judiciary's role in checking executive power and underscored the importance of judicial independence in upholding the rule of law.

Rule of Law: Governing Through Law, Not Power

The **rule of law** is a fundamental concept in constitutional law, emphasizing that all individuals, including government officials, are subject to the law. It stands in opposition to arbitrary rule, where decisions are made based on the whims of rulers rather than established legal principles.

Case Study: A.D.M. Jabalpur v. Shivkant Shukla (Habeas Corpus Case, 1976)

One of the most controversial judgments in Indian legal history, the **A.D.M. Jabalpur v. Shivkant Shukla** case, tested the rule of law during the Indian Emergency (1975-1977). The government had suspended **Article 21** of the Indian Constitution, which guarantees the right to life and personal liberty, leading to widespread arrests without due process. When petitions for **habeas corpus** were filed, the Supreme Court ruled in favor of the government, effectively allowing the suspension of fundamental rights during the Emergency.

The judgment was widely criticized for undermining the rule of law, as it permitted the state to detain individuals without judicial oversight. Justice H.R. Khanna, the sole dissenting judge, argued that "the law is above the rulers," underscoring the importance of judicial review even in times of national crisis. This case remains a stark reminder of the dangers of undermining the rule of law in favor of executive power.

Rule of Law in the International Context: Nuremberg Trials

The **Nuremberg Trials** after World War II marked a significant moment for the rule of law on the international stage. For the first time, individuals were held accountable for crimes against humanity, and the defense of "following orders" was rejected. The trials established that the rule of law applies universally, and even the highest-ranking officials are not above the law.

The principles established at Nuremberg continue to influence international law and have been invoked in subsequent trials for war crimes and genocides, including those in Rwanda and the former Yugoslavia. The Nuremberg Trials reinforced the global commitment to the rule of law as a safeguard against tyranny and injustice.

Due Process: Protecting Fairness in Law

Due process is a constitutional guarantee that the government will respect all legal rights owed to a person. It ensures that laws are applied fairly and that individuals are not deprived of life, liberty, or property without proper legal procedures. Due process is a critical element in both criminal and civil proceedings.

Substantive and Procedural Due Process

Due process can be divided into two categories:

- **Procedural Due Process**: This refers to the procedures that must be followed before depriving a person of life, liberty, or property. For example, a person must be given notice and a fair hearing before being imprisoned.

- **Substantive Due Process**: This concept focuses on whether the laws themselves are fair and just, regardless of the procedures used to enforce them.

In **Maneka Gandhi v. Union of India** (1978), the Supreme Court of India expanded the interpretation of **Article 21**, ruling that **procedural due process** must be "fair, just, and reasonable." The case involved the arbitrary impounding of Maneka Gandhi's passport, and the court held that any procedure established by law must pass the test of reasonableness, linking procedural and substantive due process under the Constitution.

U.S. Landmark Case: Brown v. Board of Education (1954)

In **Brown v. Board of Education**, the U.S. Supreme Court ruled that racial segregation in public schools violated the **Equal Protection Clause** of the Fourteenth Amendment. While the case primarily dealt with racial equality, it also reflected the principle of substantive due process by challenging the fairness of laws that allowed segregation. The decision marked a turning point in American civil rights, demonstrating how due process and equal protection work together to ensure justice.

Equal Protection: Ensuring Fair Treatment

The principle of **equal protection** mandates that individuals in similar situations must be treated equally by the law. It prevents discriminatory practices and ensures that

no person or group is given preferential treatment without a legitimate reason.

Article 14 of the Indian Constitution: Equality Before the Law

Article 14 of the Indian Constitution guarantees equality before the law and equal protection of the laws to all individuals. This principle was at the heart of the **K.S. Puttaswamy v. Union of India** (2017) case, where the Supreme Court of India declared the **right to privacy** as a fundamental right. The petitioners challenged the government's Aadhaar scheme, arguing that mandatory biometric identification violated their right to privacy and equal protection.

The court's ruling not only established privacy as a fundamental right but also emphasized that any law which treats individuals unequally must pass the test of reasonableness. The government's power to infringe upon privacy must be justified by a compelling state interest, ensuring that laws are not applied arbitrarily or discriminatorily.

Affirmative Action and Equal Protection

The concept of equal protection is also central to the debate over **affirmative action**, which aims to address historical injustices by providing advantages to historically marginalized groups. In **Regents of the University of California v. Bakke** (1978), the U.S. Supreme Court ruled on the constitutionality of race-based admissions policies. While the court struck down rigid racial quotas, it upheld the principle that race could be considered as one of many factors in university admissions to promote diversity and remedy past discrimination.

This case illustrates the delicate balance between equal protection and the need for remedial measures to achieve social justice. It highlights the complexity of applying constitutional principles in diverse, multi-cultural societies.

Judicial Review: The Power to Interpret the Constitution

Judicial review is the power of the courts to examine the constitutionality of laws and actions taken by the executive and legislative branches. This principle empowers the judiciary to strike down laws that violate the Constitution, ensuring that all branches of government operate within their constitutional limits.

Marbury v. Madison: The Birth of Judicial Review

The U.S. Supreme Court case **Marbury v. Madison** (1803) established the doctrine of judicial review, giving the judiciary the authority to strike down unconstitutional laws. This case marked the beginning of the court's role as the interpreter of the Constitution, setting a precedent that has been followed by courts around the world.

In India, judicial review is enshrined in **Article 13** of the Constitution, which states that any law inconsistent with or in derogation of the fundamental rights shall be declared void. Judicial review has been a powerful tool in protecting civil liberties and upholding the Constitution.

Case Study: Kesavananda Bharati v. State of Kerala (1973)

In **Kesavananda Bharati v. State of Kerala**, the Supreme Court of India established the **Basic Structure Doctrine**, ruling that while Parliament has the power to amend the Constitution, it cannot alter its basic structure. This landmark case cemented the judiciary's role as the guardian of the Constitution, ensuring that no amendment could undermine fundamental principles such as the rule of law, separation of powers, and judicial review itself.

The **Kesavananda** judgment illustrates the critical role of judicial review in maintaining constitutional integrity. By setting limits on the amendment power, the court ensured that the fundamental principles of the Constitution would remain inviolable, even in the face of political pressure.

Strict Scrutiny and Rational Basis: Testing the Constitutionality of Laws

When courts review the constitutionality of laws, they apply different standards of review depending on the nature of the rights involved. Two common standards are **strict scrutiny** and **rational basis review**.

Strict Scrutiny: Protecting Fundamental Rights

Strict scrutiny is the highest standard of judicial review and is applied when a law infringes upon a fundamental right or involves a suspect classification such as race or religion. Under strict scrutiny, the government must prove that the law serves a **compelling state interest** and is narrowly tailored to achieve that interest.

In **Shayara Bano v. Union of India** (2017), the Supreme Court of India applied a form of strict scrutiny to strike down the practice of **triple talaq** (instant divorce) as unconstitutional. The court ruled that the practice violated the fundamental rights of Muslim women to equality and dignity. The decision reflected the court's role in protecting fundamental rights, even when such practices were justified under religious law.

7.2 Rational Basis Review: A Lower Standard

In contrast, **rational basis review** is a more lenient standard, applied when the law does not involve a fundamental right or suspect classification. Under this test, the government only needs to show that the law is **rationally related** to a legitimate government interest.

In **Fisher v. University of Texas** (2016), the U.S. Supreme Court applied a modified form of strict scrutiny to uphold the university's affirmative action program, finding that it was narrowly tailored to achieve the compelling interest of diversity. However, the court applied rational basis review to other non-racial admissions criteria, demonstrating how different standards of review can be applied within the same case.

The Living Language of Constitutional Law

Constitutional law is not static; it evolves with each interpretation, each case, each judgment. The vocabulary we have explored in this chapter is not merely academic but reflects the living nature of constitutions, as they adapt to the changing needs of society. Terms like **sovereignty**, **due process**, and **equal protection** are not just words, they are the essence of justice, freedom, and equality.

To master constitutional law is to understand the stories these words tell: the stories of struggle, of triumph, of evolving democracies, and of the endless quest for justice.

"The Constitution is not an instrument for the government to restrain the people, it is an instrument for the people to restrain the government, lest it come to dominate our lives and interests."

\- **Patrick Henry**

Exercises and Practical Applications

1. **Case Analysis**:

Analyze a recent constitutional law case from the Supreme Court of India. Identify the key constitutional principles involved (such as sovereignty, due process, or equal protection) and discuss how the court applied these principles to reach its decision.

2. **Legal Writing Exercise**:

Draft a brief arguing that a specific law violates the principle of equal protection under Article 14 of the Indian Constitution. Use real-life examples and case law to support your argument.

3. **Oral Argument Preparation**:

Prepare an oral argument for a hypothetical case challenging a government policy on the grounds of substantive due process. Focus on articulating why the law in question fails the test of fairness and reasonableness.

By engaging with these exercises, you will deepen your understanding of constitutional law vocabulary and its practical application in real-world legal scenarios.

Chapter 8: Contract Law Vocabulary

"Contracts are the foundation of commerce. They create obligations and ensure that promises are kept. The language of contracts must be precise, clear, and unambiguous."

\- **Lord Mansfield**

The Power Behind a Promise

A contract is more than a simple exchange of promises. It is the foundation of trust, a framework that enables individuals and businesses to rely on each other, knowing that the law will uphold their agreements. The language of contract law gives structure to these relationships, and each term carries profound meaning, shaping the rights and obligations of the parties involved.

Whether it's a multi-billion dollar corporate merger or a simple purchase of goods, contracts form the backbone of economic and social transactions. But for law students and new lawyers, understanding contract law isn't just about knowing what a contract is, it's about grasping the nuances of terms like "offer," "consideration," and "breach." Each term represents a vital element in the formation, execution, and enforcement of agreements.

In this chapter, we will explore the essential vocabulary of contract law through real-life case studies, examining how courts have interpreted these terms to resolve disputes. From India's evolving contract law jurisprudence to influential cases from the UK and the US, we will dive deep into the language that drives this area of law.

Offer: The First Step Toward an Agreement

An **offer** is the first essential component of any contract. It represents a clear intention by one party to be bound by specific terms if the other party accepts. An offer must be definite, and its terms must be communicated clearly. The significance of an offer lies in the fact that it sets the stage for mutual consent, which is the bedrock of any valid contract.

Case Study: Carlill v. Carbolic Smoke Ball Co. (1893)

The classic case of **Carlill v. Carbolic Smoke Ball Co.** (1893) from the UK is a textbook example of how an offer can be structured and interpreted. The Carbolic Smoke Ball Company advertised that it would pay £100 to anyone who used its product and still contracted influenza. Mrs. Carlill used the smoke ball as instructed but fell ill. The company argued that the advertisement was not a binding offer, but the court disagreed.

The judgment held that the advertisement constituted a valid offer because it was clear, precise, and demonstrated the company's intent to be bound, especially as they had even deposited money in the bank to show their seriousness. This case illustrates that an offer can be made to the world at large and still be legally enforceable, as long as its terms are clear and specific.

Invitation to Treat: Understanding the Difference

It's important to distinguish an **offer** from an **invitation to treat**, the latter is not an offer but an invitation for others to make offers. A classic example is a display of goods in a store. The display is not an offer to sell but an invitation for customers to make an offer to buy. The shop owner can then accept or reject that offer.

In **Pharmaceutical Society of Great Britain v. Boots Cash Chemists** (1953), the court held that goods displayed on shelves in a self-service store constituted an invitation to treat, not an offer.

The offer occurred when the customer took the item to the cashier, and the contract was concluded when the cashier accepted payment.

Understanding the difference between an offer and an invitation to treat is crucial for correctly framing agreements in various contexts.

Acceptance: Binding the Agreement

Acceptance is the mirror image of the offer, signaling the offeree's agreement to the terms proposed by the offeror. For acceptance to be valid, it must be unequivocal and communicated to the offeror. Silence cannot constitute acceptance unless specifically agreed upon.

Case Study: Bhagwandas Goverdhandas Kedia v. Girdharilal Parshottamdas & Co. (1966)

In the landmark Indian case of **Bhagwandas Goverdhandas Kedia v. Girdharilal Parshottamdas & Co.**, the Supreme Court of India dealt with the issue of when and where acceptance is considered complete in contracts made by telephone or telegram. The court held that a contract is concluded where the acceptance is heard by the offeror. This case clarified the timing and location of acceptance, emphasizing that acceptance must be effectively communicated to the offeror for the contract to be binding.

The ruling reinforced the idea that acceptance must mirror the terms of the offer and must be communicated in a manner that is mutually understood by both parties. The judgment also highlights the evolving nature of communication methods in contract law, particularly as modern technology continues to reshape how agreements are made.

Counter-Offer vs. Acceptance

A **counter-offer** is not an acceptance, it's a rejection of the original offer and puts forward a new set of terms. This distinction was made clear in **Hyde v. Wrench** (1840), where Wrench offered to sell his farm to Hyde for £1,000. Hyde responded by offering £950, which Wrench refused. Hyde then tried to accept the original offer of £1,000, but the court ruled that his counter-offer had already terminated the original offer, meaning there was no contract.

This case shows how delicate the process of acceptance can be and how easily an agreement can be undone if the terms are not aligned.

Consideration: The Price of a Promise

In contract law, **consideration** refers to something of value that each party agrees to exchange. Without consideration, a contract is generally not enforceable, as it lacks the necessary element of reciprocity. The concept of consideration ensures that both parties are bound by an obligation that benefits each other.

Case Study: Chinnaya v. Ramayya (1882)

The Indian case of **Chinnaya v. Ramayya** (1882) is a critical precedent in understanding consideration. In this case, a woman gifted land to her daughter, with the stipulation that the daughter pay an annuity to her uncle. The daughter failed to make the payments, and the uncle sued. The defense argued that since the uncle had provided no consideration, there was no enforceable contract between him and the daughter.

However, the court held that consideration need not flow from the promisee but could flow from a third party. The promise was upheld, and the daughter was required to make the payments. This ruling established the principle that consideration can move from anyone, not just the parties to the contract, broadening the understanding of consideration under Indian contract law.

Past Consideration: A Contested Area

One area of complexity is **past consideration**, which is generally not valid. This means that something given or done in the past cannot be used as consideration for a present contract. However, exceptions exist, especially in cases where the service or benefit was provided with the expectation of payment.

In **Re McArdle** (1951), a woman carried out renovations on a house owned by her and her siblings. After the work was done, her siblings agreed to pay her a sum of money. When they later refused, the court ruled that the promise was not binding, as the work had been completed before the promise was made, thus, there was no valid consideration.

Understanding the nuances of consideration helps clarify when a contract becomes legally enforceable, ensuring that the promises exchanged are supported by mutual obligations.

Capacity to Contract: Who Can Make a Contract?

For a contract to be valid, the parties must have the **capacity to contract**. This means they must have the legal ability to enter into a contract, which generally excludes minors, people of unsound mind, and those disqualified by law.

Case Study: Mohori Bibee v. Dharmodas Ghose (1903)

One of the leading cases on capacity in Indian contract law is **Mohori Bibee v. Dharmodas Ghose** (1903), where a minor borrowed money by mortgaging property. The lender sued for repayment, but the court held that the contract was void because the minor did not have the capacity to contract. The Privy Council ruled that any contract entered into by a minor is void ab initio (from the beginning), not merely voidable.

This case illustrates how fundamental capacity is to contract law, protecting minors and other vulnerable individuals from being bound by legal agreements they may not fully understand or appreciate.

Free Consent: The Importance of Voluntariness

For a contract to be valid, both parties must give their consent freely. **Free consent** means that the agreement was made without coercion, undue influence, fraud, misrepresentation, or mistake. When consent is tainted by any of these factors, the contract may be voidable at the option of the party whose consent was not free.

Case Study: Ranganayakamma v. Alwar Setti (1889)

In **Ranganayakamma v. Alwar Setti** (1889), the court dealt with the issue of consent obtained under coercion. A young widow was coerced into adopting a boy by her relatives, who told her they would not cremate her deceased husband's body unless she complied. The court found that her consent was not free, as it had been obtained under undue pressure. The adoption was declared void.

This case emphasizes that consent must be voluntary and genuine for a contract to be valid. It serves as a reminder of the importance of free will in contractual agreements and the legal consequences when that free will is compromised.

Breach of Contract: The Consequences of Breaking a Promise

A **breach of contract** occurs when one party fails to fulfill their obligations under the agreement. When a breach happens, the non-breaching party is entitled to seek remedies, which may include damages, specific performance, or rescission of the contract.

Case Study: Hadley v. Baxendale (1854)

The case of **Hadley v. Baxendale** (1854) is a landmark English case that established the rule for determining damages for breach of contract. In this case, Hadley, a miller, had a broken crankshaft that needed to be repaired. He hired Baxendale to transport the shaft to the manufacturer, but Baxendale delayed, causing Hadley to lose profits as his mill remained closed. The court ruled that Hadley could only recover damages that were reasonably foreseeable at the time the contract was made.

This case established the principle that damages for breach of contract should be limited to those that both parties could have reasonably anticipated when entering the contract. This "foreseeability test" remains a cornerstone in the law of contract damages.

Remedies for Breach

The remedies for breach of contract can vary depending on the nature and terms of the contract. Common remedies include:

- **Damages**: Monetary compensation for the loss suffered due to the breach. These can be compensatory, punitive, or nominal, depending on the circumstances.

- **Specific Performance**: A court order requiring the breaching party to fulfill their contractual obligations. This remedy is often used in cases involving unique goods or property.

- **Rescission**: The cancellation of the contract, with both parties returning to their pre-contractual positions.

In the case of **Taylor v. Caldwell** (1863), the court introduced the doctrine of **frustration**, where a contract is discharged due to unforeseen circumstances that make performance impossible. In this case, a music hall burned down before a concert could be held, and the court ruled that the contract was frustrated, meaning both parties were excused from their obligations.

Understanding breach of contract and the remedies available is crucial for navigating disputes and ensuring that parties can recover or mitigate their losses.

Void and Voidable Contracts: Distinguishing Between the Two

Contracts can be either **void** or **voidable**, depending on the circumstances under which they were formed.

- A **void contract** is one that is not enforceable by law from the beginning. Examples include contracts with illegal purposes or contracts with minors, as seen in **Mohori Bibee v. Dharmodas Ghose**.

- A **voidable contract**, on the other hand, is one that is valid until one of the parties chooses to void it. This is often the case when a contract was formed under duress or fraud.

Case Study: Allcard v. Skinner (1887)

In **Allcard v. Skinner**, a nun transferred her wealth to her religious order. Years later, she left the order and sought to recover her property, arguing that she had been unduly influenced into making the transfer. The court held that while the contract was not void, it was voidable due to undue influence. However, Allcard's delay in seeking relief prevented her from recovering her property, illustrating the importance of acting promptly when seeking to void a contract.

The Precision of Promises

Contracts, at their core, are promises made enforceable by law. The vocabulary of contract law, terms like offer, acceptance, consideration, and breach, may seem technical, but they hold within them the heart of human agreements. These terms define the responsibilities we take on and the trust we place in others.

In understanding contract law, we understand not just the mechanics of promises but the depth of human intention, trust, and accountability. A well-drafted contract can protect interests, foster relationships, and ensure justice in case of a breach. As you navigate the world of contracts, remember that the law of agreements is more than rules; it is the language of trust, made legally binding.

"In a contract, as in life, the promise is sacred. But without the understanding of law, even the most sincere promise can fall apart."

\- **Justice J.S. Verma**

Exercises and Practical Applications

1. **Drafting a Contract**:

Draft a simple contract for a service agreement between a freelance graphic designer and a company. Ensure that you include clear terms related to the offer, consideration, obligations, and remedies for breach.

2. **Case Analysis**:

Analyze a recent breach of contract case from your jurisdiction. Identify the key elements that led to the breach and discuss how the court determined the appropriate remedy.

3. **Role Play Exercise**:

Imagine you are representing a client in a dispute over a voidable contract. Prepare an argument that explains why the contract should be voided, focusing on issues like undue influence or misrepresentation.

By completing these exercises, you will strengthen your understanding of contract law vocabulary and its practical applications in real-world legal contexts.

Chapter 9: Tort Law Terminology

"The law of torts exists to compensate those who have been wronged, to restore them to their original position, and to deter future wrongdoing."

- **William Prosser**

The Language of Wrongs and Responsibilities

Tort law is about human relationships, responsibility, and the consequences of our actions. It is where the law steps in to right the wrongs we do to one another, often unintentionally but with real and sometimes devastating effects. The essence of tort law can be found in its vocabulary, **negligence**, **duty of care**, **strict liability**, **damages**, each word carrying a world of meaning, each defining the boundaries of accountability in a civilized society.

Tort law, unlike criminal law, does not concern itself with punishment for moral wrongs, but with compensating those who have suffered due to the actions or inactions of others. It provides remedies for harm, ensuring that justice is served in ways that are practical, personal, and profoundly fair. Understanding the language of tort law is the key to navigating its complexities and ensuring that those who suffer injustice are properly compensated.

In this chapter, we will break down the core vocabulary of tort law, weaving through real case studies, landmark judgments, and legal principles. From negligence to intentional torts, from remedies to defenses, the language of tort law is both simple and profound, offering a clear path to justice for those who understand its nuances.

Negligence: The Heart of Modern Tort Law

At the center of tort law lies the concept of **negligence**, the failure to exercise the standard of care that a reasonable person would in a similar situation. Negligence forms the backbone of many tort cases, as it allows for accountability without requiring proof of intent. Negligence is based on the breach of a **duty of care** owed by one person to another.

Case Study: Donoghue v. Stevenson (1932)

The landmark case of **Donoghue v. Stevenson** (1932) is the foundational case for modern negligence law. In this case, Mrs. Donoghue drank from a bottle of ginger beer that contained the remains of a decomposed snail. She fell ill and sued the manufacturer, even though she had not purchased the bottle herself. The court ruled that the manufacturer owed a **duty of care** to the ultimate consumer, even if no direct contractual relationship existed.

This case established the **neighbor principle**, famously articulated by Lord Atkin: "You must take reasonable care to avoid acts or omissions which you can reasonably foresee would be likely to injure your neighbor." The "neighbor" in law refers to anyone who might reasonably be affected by your actions. The ruling in **Donoghue v. Stevenson** expanded the scope of tort law, laying the foundation for modern negligence claims worldwide.

Duty of Care: A Fundamental Concept

At the heart of negligence is the concept of **duty of care**. It refers to the legal obligation one person has to another, requiring them to act with reasonable care in certain situations. The existence of a duty is determined by the relationship between the parties and the foreseeability of harm.

In **Caparo Industries Plc v. Dickman** (1990), the UK House of Lords laid out the **Caparo test** to determine the existence of a duty of care, requiring:

1. **Foreseeability** of damage,

2. A relationship of **proximity** between the parties,

3. That it must be **fair, just, and reasonable** to impose a duty of care.

The **Caparo test** is widely applied in jurisdictions that follow common law, ensuring that duty of care is not imposed indiscriminately but is only applicable in appropriate cases.

2. Causation and Remoteness: Linking Action to Harm

Once a duty of care is established, the next step in a negligence case is proving **causation**, that the defendant's breach of duty caused the plaintiff's harm. But causation is not always straightforward. The law also requires that the harm must not be too remote from the defendant's actions, a principle known as **remoteness**.

Case Study: The Wagon Mound (No. 1) (1961)

In **Overseas Tankship (UK) Ltd v. Morts Dock and Engineering Co Ltd (The Wagon Mound No. 1)** (1961), a ship's crew negligently allowed oil to spill into Sydney Harbor. Two days later, the oil ignited, causing significant damage to a wharf. The court held that, although the crew was negligent in allowing the oil to spill, the fire was not a reasonably foreseeable consequence of their negligence. As a result, the defendants were not liable for the damage caused by the fire.

This case clarified the principle of **remoteness of damage**, establishing that a defendant is only liable for harm that is reasonably foreseeable. It emphasizes that not all consequences of negligent actions will be compensated, only those that are closely connected to the breach of duty.

But For Test and Legal Causation

Causation is typically determined using the **but for** test: but for the defendant's actions, would the harm have occurred? If the answer is no, then causation is established. However, legal causation also takes into account whether the harm was too remote or if there were intervening acts that broke the chain of causation.

In **Barnett v. Chelsea & Kensington Hospital Management Committee** (1969), a hospital was found not liable for the death of a man who had been poisoned with arsenic. Although the hospital breached its duty by failing to treat him, the court ruled that the man would have died even if he had been properly treated. The case illustrates the importance of causation in negligence claims: a breach of duty alone is not enough if the breach did not cause the harm.

Intentional Torts: Actions and Consequences

While negligence focuses on unintentional harm, **intentional torts** involve deliberate actions that cause harm. Common intentional torts include **assault**, **battery**, **false imprisonment**, and **trespass**.

Assault and Battery: The Intent to Harm

Assault is the act of creating in someone a reasonable fear or apprehension of imminent harmful or offensive contact. **Battery**, on the other hand, is the actual physical contact that follows. Both require intentional action.

In **R. v. Venna** (1976), the UK Court of Appeal held that recklessness in applying unlawful force is sufficient to constitute battery, even if the defendant did not intend to cause harm. This case expanded the definition of battery, showing that intention or recklessness can both result in liability.

Case Study: Bird v. Jones (1845)

False imprisonment involves unlawfully restricting someone's freedom of movement. In **Bird v. Jones** (1845), the plaintiff was prevented from crossing a public bridge by the defendant. Although he was physically free to leave the scene by a different route, the court held that no false imprisonment had occurred, as his overall freedom of movement had not been significantly restricted.

This case highlights the principle that false imprisonment requires complete restriction of movement, even if it is for a brief period. Understanding this distinction is crucial for cases involving claims of unlawful detention or wrongful arrest.

Strict Liability: Responsibility Without Fault

In certain situations, the law imposes **strict liability**, holding someone liable for harm even if they were not negligent or intentional in causing it. Strict liability is most often applied in cases involving inherently dangerous activities or defective products.

Case Study: Rylands v. Fletcher (1868)

The doctrine of strict liability was famously established in **Rylands v. Fletcher** (1868). In this case, the defendants built a reservoir on their land, which leaked and flooded a neighboring mine. The court held that the defendants were liable even though they were not negligent, because they had brought something dangerous onto their land that escaped and caused damage.

The **Rylands v. Fletcher** rule imposes liability on those who engage in inherently hazardous activities that pose a risk to others, regardless of whether they exercised reasonable care. The case is a cornerstone of strict liability in tort law, emphasizing that certain activities carry an inherent responsibility.

Product Liability:
A Modern Application of Strict Liability

Strict liability is also applied in **product liability** cases, where manufacturers are held responsible for defects in their products that cause harm. In **Grant v. Australian Knitting Mills** (1936), the court held that a manufacturer was strictly liable for producing underwear containing harmful chemicals, even though there was no evidence of negligence.

This case demonstrates how strict liability ensures that consumers are protected from harm caused by defective products, providing a remedy even when the manufacturer did not act negligently. It reinforces the idea that those who profit from the sale of goods should bear the risk of defects.

Defenses to Torts: Protecting Against Liability

While tort law provides remedies for those harmed, defendants are not without their defenses. Common defenses in tort law include **consent**, **self-defense**, **contributory negligence**, and **assumption of risk**.

Contributory Negligence: Sharing the Blame

In cases of **contributory negligence**, the plaintiff's own negligence contributed to the harm they suffered. If established, contributory negligence can reduce or eliminate the defendant's liability.

In **Butterfield v. Forrester** (1809), the plaintiff was riding his horse too fast and collided with a pole placed in the road by the defendant. The court ruled that the plaintiff's own reckless behavior contributed to the accident, and therefore, the defendant was not liable.

This case established the principle that plaintiffs must take reasonable care for their own safety, and failure to do so can bar recovery in negligence claims.

Volenti Non Fit Injuria: The Defense of Consent

The defense of **volenti non fit injuria** (to a willing person, no harm is done) applies when the plaintiff knowingly and voluntarily assumes the risk of harm. In **Smith v. Baker** (1891), a worker was injured by falling rocks during the course of his employment. The defendant argued that the worker had consented to the risk by continuing to work in dangerous conditions. However, the court rejected this defense, ruling that mere knowledge of danger does not constitute consent.

This case underscores that true consent must be informed and voluntary, and that workers should not be assumed to accept risks merely by remaining in hazardous employment.

Damages: Compensating for Harm

The purpose of awarding **damages** in tort law is to compensate the plaintiff for the harm they have suffered. Damages can take several forms, including **compensatory**, **punitive**, and **nominal** damages.

Compensatory Damages: Restoring the Plaintiff

Compensatory damages are intended to restore the plaintiff to the position they were in before the tort occurred. These can include both **economic** damages (such as medical expenses and lost income) and **non-economic** damages (such as pain and suffering).

In **McGregor v. Kilboy Estate** (2002), a personal injury case in Canada, the court awarded significant compensatory damages to a plaintiff who had suffered permanent disability due to a car accident. The damages covered not only medical expenses but also future loss of earning capacity, illustrating the comprehensive nature of compensatory damages in tort law.

Punitive Damages: Punishing Wrongdoers

Punitive damages go beyond compensation and are intended to punish the defendant for particularly egregious behavior. In **Rookes v. Barnard** (1964), the UK House of Lords held that punitive damages are only appropriate in cases where the defendant's conduct was oppressive, arbitrary, or unconstitutional.

Punitive damages are rare in most jurisdictions, but they serve an important purpose in deterring misconduct, particularly in cases involving deliberate harm or reckless disregard for others' safety.

Vicarious Liability: Holding Employers Responsible

Vicarious liability holds employers legally responsible for the actions of their employees, as long as those actions were committed within the scope of employment. This doctrine is based on the principle that employers should bear the costs of risks created by their business operations.

Case Study: State Bank of India v. Shyama Devi (1978)

In **State Bank of India v. Shyama Devi**, the bank was held vicariously liable for the fraudulent actions of one of its employees who had embezzled money from a customer. The court ruled that because the employee had acted within the course of his employment, the bank was responsible for the loss.

This case emphasizes that employers are not absolved of liability simply because the employee acted dishonestly. Vicarious liability ensures that businesses remain accountable for the actions of those they employ, even when those actions are wrongful.

Defamation: Protecting Reputation

Defamation occurs when one party makes false statements about another, damaging their reputation. Defamation can take two forms: **libel** (written defamation) and **slander** (spoken defamation).

Case Study: New York Times Co. v. Sullivan (1964)

In **New York Times Co. v. Sullivan**, the U.S. Supreme Court established the principle that public figures must prove "actual malice" to win defamation cases. This means they must show that the defamatory statements were made with knowledge of their falsity or with reckless disregard for the truth.

The ruling emphasized the importance of free speech, especially in matters involving public officials. It struck a balance between protecting reputations and safeguarding freedom of the press.

Tort law is a reflection of society's collective understanding of responsibility. It weaves through the fabric of everyday life, touching upon relationships, businesses, and communities. Through its vocabulary, we learn not just about rights and remedies, but about the weight of our actions and the importance of care in everything we do.

In understanding tort law, we understand a deeper truth: that every action has consequences, and that justice requires us to recognize, address, and right the wrongs we do to others.

"The law of torts is not a rigid set of rules, but a flexible and dynamic field that evolves with society, seeking to balance accountability and fairness in the face of harm."

- **Justice Y.V. Chandrachud**

Exercises and Practical Applications

1. **Mock Trial**:

Conduct a mock trial based on a negligence case involving a traffic accident. Assign roles for the plaintiff, defendant, witnesses, and judge. Focus on presenting evidence, establishing duty of care, and arguing causation.

2. **Draft a Defamation Claim**:

Imagine you are representing a client in a defamation case. Draft the initial complaint, detailing the defamatory statements, the harm caused, and the damages sought.

3. **Analyze a Landmark Case**:

Choose a landmark tort law case from your jurisdiction and analyze its impact on the development of tort law. Focus on how the case clarified key concepts such as duty of care, causation, or strict liability.

By completing these exercises, you will deepen your understanding of tort law vocabulary and gain practical experience in applying legal principles to real-world situations.

Chapter 10: Procedural Law Vocabulary

"Procedure is the handmaiden of justice. It should facilitate, not obstruct, the pursuit of truth and fairness."

\- **Justice Earl Warren**

The Architecture of Justice

The world of law is not just about principles and rights; it is about the means through which those rights are exercised and protected. This is where **procedural law** comes into play. While substantive law deals with what the law is, procedural law governs how the law is enforced. It provides the structure, the step-by-step blueprint, to ensure fairness and consistency in the judicial process.

Without procedural law, the entire legal system would be vulnerable to chaos and arbitrariness. Whether you're bringing a case to court or defending against a claim, understanding the vocabulary of procedural law is essential. Terms like **jurisdiction**, **venue**, **standing**, and **statute of limitations** may seem dry on the surface, but they represent the very lifeblood of legal practice. They dictate where a case can be heard, who can bring a claim, and how long one has to seek justice.

In this chapter, we will explore these key procedural law terms through real-world cases and precedents, focusing on how courts, both in India and abroad, have interpreted and applied them. These terms, though technical, shape the paths through which justice is accessed. Through their understanding, we unlock the process that turns disputes into resolutions, wrongs into rights.

Jurisdiction: The Power to Adjudicate

Jurisdiction refers to the legal authority of a court to hear and decide a case. Without jurisdiction, a court's decision is void. Jurisdiction can be based on various factors, such as geography, the subject matter of the dispute, or the status of the parties involved.

Case Study: A.K. Gopalan v. State of Madras (1950)

In **A.K. Gopalan v. State of Madras**, the Supreme Court of India dealt with the concept of **jurisdiction** in a case involving preventive detention. Gopalan challenged his detention under the Preventive Detention Act, arguing that it violated his fundamental rights. The court, however, upheld his detention, stating that the preventive detention law fell within the jurisdiction of the state legislature and that the court could not interfere unless the procedure prescribed by law was not followed.

This case illustrated the principle that jurisdiction involves both the court's power and the legislative competence to enact laws. **Gopalan** also opened the discussion on the relationship between procedural safeguards and substantive rights, setting the stage for future debates on due process in India.

Subject-Matter Jurisdiction: Limits on Power

Subject-matter jurisdiction refers to the court's authority to hear cases of a particular type. For example, family courts hear divorce cases, while criminal courts handle offenses like theft and assault.

In **Marbury v. Madison** (1803), a U.S. Supreme Court decision, the court established the principle of **judicial review**, but also declared that it lacked jurisdiction to grant Marbury's request for a writ of mandamus, as the case did not fall within the original jurisdiction granted to the Supreme Court by the U.S. Constitution. The case defined the limits of the court's power and illustrated how jurisdiction serves as a gatekeeper to legal claims.

Venue: Where the Case Is Heard

Venue refers to the physical location where a case is heard. While jurisdiction is about whether a court has the authority to hear a case, venue is about the most appropriate location for that hearing.

Case Study: Karti P. Chidambaram v. Directorate of Enforcement (2019)

In this high-profile Indian case, Karti Chidambaram, son of former Union Minister P. Chidambaram, challenged the **venue** of his trial under the Prevention of Money Laundering Act (PMLA). He argued that the case should be heard in Chennai, where the alleged crime occurred, rather than Delhi, where the Enforcement Directorate had filed the charge sheet. However, the court ruled that the case could be tried in Delhi, emphasizing that venue is not just about where the crime happened but where the proceedings can best be managed.

The ruling highlighted the discretionary nature of venue decisions in Indian law, where public interest, convenience, and the availability of evidence can influence where a case is heard.

Forum Non Conveniens: When Venue Is Inconvenient

In the doctrine of **forum non conveniens**, a court may refuse to hear a case if it believes that another venue is more appropriate. This principle was applied in **Spiliada Maritime Corp v. Cansulex Ltd** (1987), where the UK House of Lords ruled that a case could be dismissed if another court had a more substantial connection to the dispute. The decision underlines how venue is about finding a forum that serves justice efficiently, considering the location of evidence, witnesses, and parties.

Standing: The Right to Bring a Case

Standing refers to the legal right of a person to initiate a lawsuit. A plaintiff must have a direct interest in the matter and must demonstrate how they have been affected by the defendant's actions.

Case Study: S.P. Gupta v. Union of India (1981)

The concept of **locus standi**, or standing, was dramatically expanded in **S.P. Gupta v. Union of India**, a landmark case that opened the doors for **public interest litigation** (PIL) in India. Justice P.N. Bhagwati held that in cases involving public interest, anyone who has sufficient interest in the matter can file a petition, even if they are not directly affected.

This case transformed the Indian legal landscape by empowering individuals and organizations to file cases on behalf of disadvantaged or marginalized groups. It marked a departure from the traditional rule of standing, making justice more accessible and inclusive.

Standing in U.S. Law: Lujan v. Defenders of Wildlife (1992)

In the U.S., standing is more rigidly defined. In **Lujan v. Defenders of Wildlife**, the U.S. Supreme Court ruled that environmental activists did not have standing to challenge government actions that threatened endangered species abroad because they could not demonstrate a personal injury that was concrete and particularized. The court emphasized that plaintiffs must show a direct connection to the harm they are alleging.

This case contrasts with the liberal approach to standing in India, showing how different legal systems interpret the right to bring a lawsuit in vastly different ways.

Statute of Limitations: Time Limits on Legal Action

The **statute of limitations** refers to the time frame within which a lawsuit must be filed. After this period has passed, the plaintiff loses the right to bring a case. The rationale behind statutes of limitations is to prevent the indefinite threat of legal action and ensure that cases are brought while evidence is fresh.

Case Study: N. Balakrishnan v. M. Krishnamurthy (1998)

In **N. Balakrishnan v. M. Krishnamurthy**, the Supreme Court of India addressed the issue of delayed filings. The court held that a delay in filing a suit could be condoned if the plaintiff could provide a reasonable explanation for the delay. This case demonstrated that while statutes of limitations are important, courts have the discretion to allow late filings in the interest of justice.

The ruling also introduced the concept of **condonation of delay**, which allows flexibility in procedural timelines if the delay is justified by the circumstances.

Discovering the Cause of Action: Latent Injury Cases

In some cases, plaintiffs may not immediately be aware of the harm caused by the defendant's actions. This is common in cases of medical malpractice or toxic exposure. Many jurisdictions provide for **discovery rules**, where the statute of limitations begins when the plaintiff discovers or reasonably should have discovered the injury.

In **Cartledge v. E Jopling & Sons Ltd** (1963), workers who contracted lung disease from asbestos exposure were allowed to file claims even though the damage had occurred years earlier. The court held that the statute of limitations began when the workers first became aware of their illness. The decision underscores how the law accommodates hidden or long-term injuries to ensure justice is served.

Pleadings: Framing the Issues of the Case

Pleadings are the written documents that initiate a lawsuit and define the issues to be decided by the court. They include the **complaint**, **answer**, and in some cases, a **counterclaim** or **cross-complaint**. The precision and clarity of pleadings are critical, as they set the foundation for the trial.

Case Study: Chhotey Lal v. Chhitam Pandey (1984)

In **Chhotey Lal v. Chhitam Pandey**, the Supreme Court of India emphasized the importance of precise pleadings in civil cases. The plaintiff had filed a vague complaint, failing to specify the facts necessary to establish a legal cause of action. The court ruled that the lack of clarity in the pleadings was fatal to the case.

This case illustrates the principle that pleadings must be detailed and specific, outlining all material facts and legal grounds for the claim. In civil litigation, pleadings serve as the roadmap for the trial, and any omissions or ambiguities can derail the plaintiff's case.

Amending Pleadings: A Second Chance

Courts generally allow parties to **amend** their pleadings if new facts arise or if the original pleadings contain errors. However, there are limits to this flexibility. In **Panchdeo Narain Srivastava v. Km. Jyoti Sahay** (1983), the Indian Supreme Court held that while pleadings can be amended in the interest of justice, amendments should not introduce new claims that fundamentally alter the nature of the case.

This case highlights the balance between ensuring that the court hears the case on its merits and preventing parties from using amendments to manipulate the proceedings.

Motion: Requests for Court Action

A **motion** is a formal request made to the court for a specific ruling or order. Motions can be made at any stage of the litigation process, and they often play a crucial role in shaping the course of the trial.

Case Study: Monsanto Co. v. Coramandal Indag Products (1986)

In the case of **Monsanto Co. v. Coramandal Indag Products**, the plaintiffs filed a **motion for injunction**, seeking to prevent the defendant from infringing on their patented agricultural product. The court granted the injunction, restraining the defendant from manufacturing or selling the disputed product pending trial.

Motions for injunctions are powerful tools in procedural law, allowing plaintiffs to seek immediate relief to prevent ongoing harm. This case demonstrated the strategic use of motions to secure temporary remedies before the trial even begins.

Summary Judgment: Avoiding Unnecessary Trials

One of the most powerful procedural tools is the **motion for summary judgment**. In this motion, a party argues that there are no genuine issues of material fact requiring a trial, and that they are entitled to judgment as a matter of law. Summary judgment can save time and resources by resolving cases without a full trial.

In **Celotex Corp. v. Catrett** (1986), the U.S. Supreme Court clarified the standard for summary judgment, holding that the party moving for summary judgment need not prove the absence of issues of material fact, but simply point to the absence of evidence supporting the other party's claim. This decision strengthened the use of summary judgment, streamlining the litigation process by weeding out cases with insufficient evidence.

Discovery: Uncovering the Evidence

Discovery is the pre-trial process through which parties obtain evidence from each other. The purpose of discovery is to prevent surprises at trial, allowing both parties to prepare their cases based on full knowledge of the facts.

Case Study: Satyam Computer Services Scandal

In the Satyam scandal, one of India's biggest corporate fraud cases, discovery played a crucial role. The **disclosure** of internal emails, financial documents, and audit reports during the discovery process helped prosecutors build a strong case against the company's executives. This case underscores how discovery allows parties to uncover critical evidence that may not be voluntarily disclosed.

Types of Discovery: Depositions, Interrogatories, and Requests for Documents

- **Depositions** are sworn statements given by witnesses before trial.

- **Interrogatories** are written questions that one party sends to another, requiring written answers under oath.

- **Requests for Documents** compel the opposing party to produce specific documents relevant to the case.

In **Hickman v. Taylor** (1947), the U.S. Supreme Court ruled on the scope of discovery, holding that while discovery is broad, certain materials, such as attorney work products, are protected from disclosure. This case established important limits on discovery, ensuring that while parties are entitled to evidence, some documents remain privileged.

Appeals: Seeking a Second Opinion

Once a trial concludes and a judgment is entered, the losing party may file an **appeal** to a higher court, seeking to overturn the decision. Appeals are based on legal errors made during the trial, rather than factual disputes.

Case Study: Kesavananda Bharati v. State of Kerala (1973)

The **Kesavananda Bharati v. State of Kerala** case is one of the most significant appeals in Indian legal history. The Supreme Court's decision established the **basic structure doctrine**, ruling that while Parliament has wide powers to amend the Constitution, it cannot alter its basic structure. The case was a result of an appeal challenging the government's amendments to property rights and other fundamental constitutional principles.

The appellate process in **Kesavananda Bharati** showed how appeals serve not just to correct errors but to shape constitutional jurisprudence. It demonstrated the appellate courts' role in protecting the core values of a legal system, often going beyond the narrow facts of the case.

Burden of Proof: Proving Your Case

The **burden of proof** determines which party is responsible for proving the facts of the case. In civil cases, the burden of proof is usually on the plaintiff, and the standard is the **preponderance of evidence**, meaning the plaintiff must prove that their version of events is more likely than not true. In criminal cases, the standard is **beyond a reasonable doubt**, placing a heavier burden on the prosecution.

Case Study: Woolmington v. DPP (1935)

In **Woolmington v. Director of Public Prosecutions**, the House of Lords famously ruled that the burden of proof in criminal cases rests on the prosecution. The court held that it is the prosecution's duty to prove the defendant's guilt beyond a reasonable doubt, and the defendant is presumed innocent until proven guilty. This principle, known as the **golden thread of English law**, is fundamental to the criminal justice system.

The ruling in **Woolmington** reinforced the protection of individual liberty, ensuring that no person can be convicted unless the prosecution meets the highest standard of proof.

The Blueprint of Justice

Procedural law may seem like the mechanical part of the legal process, but it is what holds the promise of justice together. Without procedure, the most profound rights would remain hollow, unprotected by the proper channels for their enforcement. Whether it's determining which court has jurisdiction, the timeline within which a case must be filed, or the burden of proof at trial, procedural law ensures that justice is not just an abstract ideal but a lived reality.

Procedural law, in its essence, creates the **path to fairness**. It is the unsung hero of the legal system, shaping every decision and ensuring that justice is served with order and precision.

"Justice is the constant and perpetual will to allot to every man his due. But without the law's procedure, this will remains only a hope."

\- **Ulpian (Roman Jurist)**

Exercises and Practical Applications

1. Jurisdiction Quiz:

List different types of jurisdiction (personal, subject-matter, territorial) and provide examples of cases where each type was crucial in determining the outcome.

2. Motion for Summary Judgment:

Draft a hypothetical motion for summary judgment in a breach of contract case. Provide facts, legal arguments, and reasons why the court should grant the motion.

3. Discovery Strategy:

In a hypothetical personal injury case, outline a strategy for discovery. Include a list of documents to request, depositions to take, and interrogatories to send to the opposing party.

Through these exercises, you will deepen your understanding of procedural law and its role in shaping legal outcomes, preparing you for the complexities of litigation and trial work.

Chapter 11: The Language of Evidence

"Evidence is the currency of the law. It is what we use to buy truth in the marketplace of justice."

- **John Henry Wigmore**

The Silent Power of Evidence

What is truth without proof? In the legal arena, mere words hold little weight unless they are supported by evidence. Evidence is the heart of every case, the foundation upon which the entire structure of justice rests. Without it, even the most righteous claims fade into obscurity. But evidence is more than just information, it is the difference between victory and defeat, between freedom and conviction.

The **language of evidence** is unique. It doesn't just involve facts; it requires a deep understanding of rules, relevance, admissibility, and procedure. Every piece of evidence must pass through the crucible of legal scrutiny before it can speak its truth. And this process, from collection to presentation, is what gives evidence its profound importance in legal systems around the world.

In this chapter, we will journey into the world of evidence, unraveling the key concepts that guide its use in courtrooms. From **admissibility** to **hearsay**, from **direct evidence** to **circumstantial evidence**, we will explore how evidence turns abstract arguments into concrete judgments. Real-world case studies from India, the United States, and other legal systems will illustrate these principles in action.

Admissibility: The Gatekeeper of Evidence

Not all evidence that is relevant to a case can be presented in court. For evidence to be considered, it must pass the test of **admissibility**. Admissibility ensures that the evidence is both **relevant** and **competent**, that is, it must have a direct bearing on the case and must be legally acceptable in the form it is presented.

Case Study: State of U.P. v. Raj Narain (1975)

One of the landmark cases dealing with the admissibility of evidence is **State of U.P. v. Raj Narain** (1975). This case, which involved allegations of election malpractices against then Prime Minister Indira Gandhi, hinged on the admissibility of confidential documents. The court had to decide whether documents protected by the Official Secrets Act could be used as evidence. In its ruling, the Supreme Court of India held that while confidentiality was important, it could not override the need for justice, and the documents were admitted as evidence.

This case established that even confidential information could be admitted in court if it was critical to the case, thus highlighting the balance between state security and the pursuit of justice.

Relevance and Competence

For evidence to be admissible, it must be **relevant**, meaning it should make the existence of any fact more or less probable than it would be without the evidence. In **Pakala Narayana Swami v. Emperor** (1939), a case involving a murder trial, the admissibility of a statement made by the deceased before his death was contested. The Privy Council ruled that the statement was admissible because it was relevant to the facts in issue, marking an important precedent in understanding relevance in Indian evidence law.

Competence, on the other hand, refers to the legal ability of the evidence to be admitted. For instance, hearsay evidence is generally considered incompetent unless it falls under an exception.

Hearsay: The Perils of Secondhand Information

One of the most misunderstood and complex areas of evidence law is **hearsay**. Hearsay refers to statements made outside the courtroom that are presented in court to prove the truth of the matter asserted. In general, hearsay is inadmissible because it lacks the reliability of direct testimony.

Case Study: Subramaniam v. Public Prosecutor (1956)

In **Subramaniam v. Public Prosecutor**, a case from Malaysia, the accused argued that his confession had been coerced by terrorists who threatened his life. The prosecution objected to this statement as hearsay. However, the Privy Council held that the statement was admissible, not to prove the truth of the threat, but to show its effect on the accused's state of mind.

This case illustrates an important exception to the hearsay rule: statements that are not offered for the truth of the matter asserted but for another purpose (such as showing the effect on the listener) may be admissible.

Exceptions to the Hearsay Rule

While hearsay is generally inadmissible, there are several exceptions where hearsay can be admitted as evidence. These include:

- **Dying Declarations**: In **Queen Empress v. Abdullah** (1885), the court accepted a dying declaration as admissible evidence. The reasoning behind this exception is that a person on the verge of death is unlikely to lie.

- **Statements Against Interest**: A statement that is against the declarant's own interest can also be admitted as an exception to the hearsay rule. This exception was applied in **Lily Thomas v. Union of India** (2000), where the court considered statements made by politicians that were against their own interests.

These exceptions ensure that valuable evidence is not excluded simply because it was made outside the courtroom, provided there are strong indications of reliability.

Direct and Circumstantial Evidence: Different Routes to the Truth

Evidence can be categorized into two main types: **direct evidence** and **circumstantial evidence**. Both have their place in courtrooms, and contrary to popular belief, circumstantial evidence can be just as powerful as direct evidence.

Direct Evidence

Direct evidence refers to testimony or material that directly proves a fact without the need for inference. For example, an eyewitness account of a crime is direct evidence. In **R v. Turnbull** (1977), the UK courts emphasized the importance of caution in accepting eyewitness testimony, noting the dangers of misidentification even in direct evidence.

Circumstantial Evidence: Connecting the Dots

Circumstantial evidence, on the other hand, requires the court to draw inferences. In many cases, circumstantial evidence can form the bulk of the prosecution's case. In **Bodh Raj v. State of Jammu and Kashmir** (2002), the Supreme Court of India famously upheld a conviction based entirely on circumstantial evidence, stating that if the chain of circumstances is so complete that it leads to the only possible conclusion of guilt, then circumstantial evidence is as good as direct evidence.

The power of circumstantial evidence lies in its ability to paint a comprehensive picture, even when direct evidence is unavailable. It reminds us that truth is often found in the connections between seemingly unrelated facts.

Documentary and Physical Evidence: Tangible Proof

While much of the evidence presented in court comes in the form of testimony, **documentary evidence** and **physical evidence** also play critical roles. These forms of evidence provide objective, tangible proof of facts.

Documentary Evidence: The Written Word

Documentary evidence includes contracts, emails, letters, and official records. In **Mohd. Yusuf v. D** (2001), the Indian Supreme Court dealt with the issue of forgery in documentary evidence. The court held that a document's authenticity must be proven before it can be admitted into evidence. This case demonstrated the importance of verifying the origin and accuracy of documentary evidence, as even a small discrepancy can undermine an entire case.

Physical Evidence: The Silent Witness

Physical evidence, also known as **real evidence**, includes objects like weapons, clothing, and fingerprints. In the **Arushi Talwar murder case**, physical evidence played a crucial role. The forensic analysis of bloodstains and DNA samples provided critical information, although the handling of the evidence was later criticized for undermining the prosecution's case.

Physical evidence, when properly handled, can speak louder than words, offering objective insights that human testimony may fail to provide.

Forensic Evidence: Science in the Courtroom

In modern trials, **forensic evidence** is increasingly important, providing scientific backing to claims made by either side. From DNA testing to ballistic analysis, forensic evidence offers objective, often irrefutable proof of facts.

Case Study: DNA Evidence in the Nirbhaya Rape Case

In the **Nirbhaya gang rape and murder case** (2012), forensic evidence played a decisive role in securing the convictions of the accused. DNA samples collected from the crime scene matched the DNA of the accused, leaving no room for doubt. The introduction of forensic science into this case transformed what could have been a circumstantial case into one backed by solid scientific evidence.

DNA, fingerprints, and other forensic evidence have become pillars in the legal system, ensuring that justice is served with a degree of certainty that was not possible in the past.

The Chain of Custody: Protecting Forensic Integrity

However, forensic evidence is only as good as the **chain of custody**. The chain of custody refers to the documentation that tracks the possession, handling, and location of evidence from the time it is collected until it is presented in court. If the chain of custody is broken, the evidence may be compromised.

In the **1995 O.J. Simpson trial** in the United States, the defense successfully challenged the handling of blood evidence, arguing that the chain of custody had been broken. This doubt cast on the forensic evidence played a significant role in Simpson's acquittal, showing that even the strongest evidence can be undermined if not properly managed.

The Burden of Proof: Proving the Case

In any trial, the **burden of proof** lies on the party bringing the case, typically the prosecution in a criminal trial or the plaintiff in a civil trial. The burden of proof dictates who must prove the facts of the case and to what degree.

Criminal Cases: Beyond a Reasonable Doubt

In criminal cases, the burden of proof is **beyond a reasonable doubt**, the highest standard in law. This standard was applied in **State of Maharashtra v. Sukhdeo Singh** (1992), where the Supreme Court of India stressed that every element of the offense must be proven beyond a reasonable doubt to secure a conviction. This high standard protects individuals from being convicted based on insufficient or ambiguous evidence.

Civil Cases: Preponderance of the Evidence

In civil cases, the burden of proof is typically the **preponderance of the evidence**. This means that the plaintiff must show that it is more likely than not that their claims are true. In **Lillie v. Director of Public Prosecutions** (2002), a UK case, the court held that in defamation suits, the plaintiff must prove the defamatory statement was made, and the defendant may have the burden to prove it was not defamatory.

These different standards of proof reflect the varying consequences in criminal and civil trials, ensuring that the level of certainty required aligns with the severity of the outcome.

Exclusionary Rules: Keeping Evidence Out

Not all evidence that is relevant and reliable will be admitted in court. Certain rules exist to exclude evidence, even when it could be valuable in determining the truth. These rules aim to ensure fairness in the trial process.

The Fruit of the Poisonous Tree Doctrine

The **fruit of the poisonous tree** doctrine is an exclusionary rule in U.S. law that prevents evidence obtained through illegal means from being used in court. This doctrine was applied in **Mapp v. Ohio** (1961), where evidence obtained from an illegal search was excluded, even though it directly implicated the defendant in a crime. This rule ensures that law enforcement does not benefit from violating constitutional rights, even if the evidence they collect is conclusive.

Indian Exclusionary Rules: Confessions to Police

Under Indian law, **Section 25 of the Indian Evidence Act, 1872** excludes confessions made to police officers from being admitted in court. This rule was upheld in **Nandini Satpathy v. P.L. Dani** (1978), where the Supreme Court of India reiterated that such confessions are inadmissible due to the potential for coercion. This exclusionary rule protects accused individuals from being unfairly pressured into making incriminating statements.

Exclusionary rules serve as checks on overreach by law enforcement and help maintain the integrity of the judicial process.

Judicial Notice: Facts That Don't Need Proof

In certain cases, courts can accept certain facts as **judicial notice**, meaning they are so well known or established that they do not require proof. For instance, the existence of a public holiday or the fact that water freezes at 0°C are facts that courts can take judicial notice of.

Case Study: State of Gujarat v. Shantilal Mangaldas (1969)

In **State of Gujarat v. Shantilal Mangaldas**, the Supreme Court of India took judicial notice of the fact that the monsoon season in Gujarat often causes floods. This fact, though not proven by specific evidence, was so widely known that it was unnecessary to prove it in court.

Judicial notice allows courts to expedite trials by not requiring proof of facts that are beyond dispute. However, the scope of judicial notice is limited to facts that are generally known or easily verifiable.

The courtroom is a stage where truth and lies clash, where justice is pursued with determination, and where the rules of evidence dictate the dance. Evidence, in all its forms, speaks louder than any argument. It holds the power to sway, to convict, to absolve. But this power is tempered by strict rules and procedures designed to ensure that only the most reliable, relevant, and fair evidence finds its way before the judge or jury.

The language of evidence, though technical, is ultimately about truth. It is about presenting the reality of what happened in a way that the legal system can understand and act upon. Through understanding how evidence operates, what is admissible, what is excluded, and how it must be proven, lawyers gain the tools they need to build strong cases and advocate effectively for justice.

"In the end, evidence is not just about proving facts; it is about uncovering the truth that lies beneath the surface. In the pursuit of justice, truth must not only be sought but also proved."

\- **Justice J.S. Verma**

Exercises and Practical Applications

1. Admissibility Debate:

Choose a controversial piece of evidence from a real or hypothetical case. Argue whether it should be admitted based on the rules of relevance, competence, and hearsay.

2. Chain of Custody Exercise:

In a mock criminal case, simulate the collection and handling of forensic evidence. Document the chain of custody and discuss what could go wrong if it is not followed properly.

3. Burden of Proof Simulation:

Conduct a mock trial with both a criminal case and a civil case. Focus on the different burdens of proof and how they influence the strategies of the prosecution and defense.

These exercises will deepen your understanding of the intricacies of evidence law and enhance your ability to navigate the complex world of trials and courtroom advocacy.

Chapter 12: Administrative and Regulatory Law Vocabulary

"Administrative law is the law of those who govern. It exists to ensure that power is exercised lawfully and that citizens are protected from arbitrary action."

\- **Lord Diplock**

The Machinery of Governance

At the heart of modern governance lies a network of regulations, agencies, and rules, an invisible machinery that keeps society running smoothly. This is the world of **administrative and regulatory law**, where governments manage everything from public safety to economic fairness. It is a domain of law that governs the regulators themselves, ensuring that the powers given to government bodies are not abused and that they function within the limits of law.

Unlike the more visible areas of criminal or constitutional law, administrative and regulatory law operates in the background, overseeing the relationships between individuals, corporations, and the state. But make no mistake: the vocabulary of administrative law is as critical as any other field. Terms like **regulation**, **agency**, **rulemaking**, **adjudication**, and **compliance** define the way governments enforce laws and ensure that public interests are protected.

This chapter explores the essential vocabulary of administrative and regulatory law, using real-world case studies and precedents to illustrate how these terms are applied in practice. We will delve into the intricacies of government agencies and regulatory bodies, understanding how they create and enforce rules, resolve disputes, and ensure that justice and fairness are upheld. Through this, you will learn how administrative law is not just a set of dry rules but a dynamic and powerful force shaping societies.

Regulation: The Rules that Shape Society

At the core of administrative law is the concept of **regulation**, a form of legal rule or directive issued by government agencies, intended to manage behaviors, enforce laws, and ensure societal order. Regulations often carry the force of law, meaning they must be followed just like any other law.

Case Study: Maneka Gandhi v. Union of India (1978)

One of the landmark cases in Indian regulatory law is **Maneka Gandhi v. Union of India**. This case challenged the government's decision to impound Maneka Gandhi's passport under the **Passport Act, 1967**, without providing her with adequate reasoning or the opportunity to be heard. The Supreme Court of India held that even administrative actions must adhere to the principles of natural justice, especially when they affect fundamental rights. This ruling reinforced the principle that regulations, though essential, must be implemented in ways that respect due process and individual liberties.

The court's decision was a turning point, setting the precedent that all regulations and administrative actions must pass the test of fairness and reasonableness, even if they serve a public interest.

Types of Regulations: Economic and Social

Regulations come in many forms, broadly categorized as **economic regulations** (which govern industries and markets) and **social regulations** (which protect health, safety, and the environment). Economic regulations might include rules set by the **Securities and Exchange Board of India (SEBI)** to govern stock market activities, while social regulations might include standards issued by the **Central Pollution Control Board (CPCB)** to limit environmental pollution.

Understanding these distinctions is crucial because they highlight how regulation is not just about control, it is about creating balance, promoting fairness, and protecting the public good.

Agency: The Instruments of Regulation

The power to regulate is often delegated to **agencies**, specialized government bodies created to enforce laws and ensure that specific policies are implemented effectively. Agencies operate within the framework of laws passed by the legislature, but they often have significant discretion in how they enforce these laws.

Case Study: Vishaka v. State of Rajasthan (1997)

The **Vishaka v. State of Rajasthan** case highlighted the role of regulatory agencies in addressing workplace harassment. In the absence of specific legislation governing sexual harassment at the workplace, the Supreme Court of India issued guidelines based on international conventions. These guidelines placed responsibility on employers, enforced through regulatory agencies, to prevent and redress sexual harassment. The court held that in the absence of legislative action, courts and regulatory bodies must ensure that fundamental rights are protected.

This case demonstrates how agencies often step in to fill gaps in legislation, using their rulemaking powers to enforce critical protections.

The Role of Agencies: Rulemaking and Enforcement

Agencies perform two essential functions: **rulemaking** and **enforcement**. **Rulemaking** refers to the process by which agencies create regulations, while **enforcement** involves ensuring compliance with these regulations. For example, the **Food Safety and Standards Authority of India (FSSAI)** creates rules about food safety and then inspects businesses to ensure that these rules are followed.

Agencies act as the hands and feet of the law, interpreting broad legislative directives and turning them into concrete rules that govern everyday life. However, they must always act within the limits of the law, respecting both their mandate and the rights of individuals.

Rulemaking: Crafting the Framework

Rulemaking is the process through which regulatory agencies create new regulations. It is one of the most important functions of an administrative body because it turns broad legislative directives into specific rules that can be applied in practice.

Case Study: SEBI and Insider Trading

A well-known example of rulemaking in India is the **Securities and Exchange Board of India (SEBI)**'s regulations on insider trading. Insider trading involves the buying or selling of securities based on confidential, non-public information, and it is illegal because it gives an unfair advantage to certain individuals. SEBI has crafted detailed regulations under the **SEBI Act, 1992** to prevent and punish insider trading.

In the case of **Rakesh Agarwal v. SEBI (2003)**, SEBI took enforcement action against an individual accused of insider trading. The case went on to clarify the scope of SEBI's powers in preventing market abuse and how rulemaking allows agencies to protect public trust in financial markets.

Procedural Safeguards in Rulemaking

Agencies must follow **procedural safeguards** when making rules to ensure transparency and accountability. For instance, under the **Administrative Procedure Act (APA)** in the United States, agencies must publish proposed rules in advance and allow public comment before the rules are finalized. This process, known as **notice-and-comment rulemaking**, ensures that stakeholders have a say in the development of regulations.

The principles of fairness and accountability apply to rulemaking globally. In **Gorkha Security Services v. Govt of NCT of Delhi (2014)**, the Indian Supreme Court emphasized the need for clear communication and transparency in administrative decisions, affirming that rulemaking and enforcement must follow due process to be valid.

Adjudication: Resolving Regulatory Disputes

When disputes arise under a regulatory framework, agencies often act as **adjudicators**, resolving issues between individuals, companies, and the state. This process is known as **administrative adjudication**, and it allows regulatory agencies to enforce compliance and settle disputes without requiring a full judicial trial.

Case Study: Telecom Regulatory Authority of India (TRAI)

The **Telecom Regulatory Authority of India (TRAI)** is a prime example of a regulatory body that frequently engages in adjudication. In **Bharti Airtel Ltd. v. TRAI (2016)**, the telecom giant challenged TRAI's regulations requiring compensation for dropped calls. Airtel argued that the rule was unfair and beyond TRAI's regulatory power. The Supreme Court ruled in favor of

Airtel, stating that the regulation was unreasonable and did not fall within the scope of TRAI's powers.

This case illustrates the important role of adjudication in holding regulatory bodies accountable for their decisions. Regulatory agencies must ensure that their actions are fair, reasonable, and within the limits of their authority.

Tribunals and Specialized Courts

In many countries, specialized courts or **tribunals** handle administrative and regulatory disputes. These bodies often provide quicker and more expert resolution than traditional courts. For example, the **National Green Tribunal (NGT)** in India deals with cases related to environmental protection, balancing the need for industrial development with the preservation of natural resources.

Tribunals like the NGT ensure that regulatory bodies remain accountable, providing a forum for individuals to challenge unfair or illegal administrative actions.

Compliance: Following the Rules

Compliance refers to the obligation of individuals, businesses, and organizations to follow the rules and regulations set by administrative bodies. Non-compliance can result in penalties, fines, or other sanctions, making compliance a critical aspect of regulatory law.

Case Study: Vodafone India v. Union of India (2012)

In one of the most significant tax disputes in India, **Vodafone India** challenged the government's attempt to impose a tax on its acquisition of an Indian company. The case revolved around the interpretation of **tax compliance** rules and whether Vodafone was required to pay taxes on the transaction. The Supreme Court ruled in favor of Vodafone, holding that the transaction did not attract tax liability under Indian law. This case highlighted the complexity of regulatory compliance in the context of cross-border transactions.

The Importance of Regulatory Compliance

Regulatory compliance extends across industries, from environmental regulations that companies must follow to ensure they do not harm the environment, to financial regulations that prevent fraud and ensure market integrity. Agencies like SEBI, the Reserve Bank of India (RBI), and the Central Pollution Control Board (CPCB) are tasked with monitoring compliance, conducting audits, and imposing penalties on those who violate the rules.

For businesses, ensuring compliance is not just about avoiding penalties; it is about maintaining trust and integrity in their operations. Effective compliance programs help companies navigate the complex web of regulations while reducing the risk of legal disputes.

Licensing and Permits: Gateways to Legal Operation

One of the primary tools of regulatory agencies is the power to grant or deny **licenses** and **permits**. These legal authorizations allow individuals or companies to engage in specific activities that are otherwise restricted by law.

Case Study: Coca-Cola's Water Usage in Kerala

In a notable case involving licensing and environmental regulations, the **Kerala High Court** addressed Coca-Cola's use of groundwater for its bottling plant in Plachimada, Kerala. Local residents claimed that excessive water extraction by Coca-Cola had caused severe water shortages. The court ruled that Coca-Cola's license to extract water could be restricted if it violated environmental laws and public interest.

This case demonstrated how licensing can be used as a regulatory tool to ensure that businesses operate in a way that does not harm the public or the environment.

The Role of Licensing in Ensuring Standards

Licenses and permits serve as a way for the government to ensure that certain standards are met before businesses can operate. For example, the **Food Safety and Standards Authority of India (FSSAI)** requires food businesses to obtain licenses that confirm they meet hygiene and safety standards. Similarly, the **Directorate General of Civil Aviation (DGCA)** issues licenses to airlines, ensuring they comply with safety regulations.

By issuing licenses, regulatory agencies maintain oversight and ensure that industries function in a manner that protects public health, safety, and welfare.

Enforcement: Upholding the Rule of Law

While rulemaking is about creating regulations, **enforcement** ensures that these regulations are followed. Regulatory agencies often have enforcement powers that allow them to impose fines, revoke licenses, and take legal action against violators.

Case Study: Environmental Enforcement by the NGT

The **National Green Tribunal (NGT)** has been instrumental in enforcing environmental regulations across India. In the **Sterlite Copper Case** (2018), the NGT upheld the Tamil Nadu Pollution Control Board's decision to close the Sterlite copper plant in Tuticorin due to environmental violations. The court ruled that the company had failed to comply with environmental standards, and the plant's operations were causing harm to the local population.

The case showcased how regulatory enforcement can protect public health and the environment from corporate malfeasance.

Penalties and Sanctions

Regulatory bodies often impose **penalties** for non-compliance, ranging from monetary fines to the suspension of operations. The **Reserve Bank of India (RBI)**, for instance, has the power to impose fines on banks that fail to meet regulatory standards. Similarly, SEBI can ban individuals or companies from participating in the securities market if they engage in fraudulent practices.

Enforcement actions ensure that regulations are not just words on paper, they are actively implemented and followed. By holding individuals and companies accountable, regulatory bodies maintain the integrity of the legal system and the markets they oversee.

Judicial Review: The Limits of Administrative Power

Judicial review is the process by which courts oversee the actions of administrative and regulatory bodies, ensuring that they do not exceed their legal powers or violate the rights of individuals. It serves as a critical check on the powers of regulatory agencies.

Case Study: Minerva Mills v. Union of India (1980)

In **Minerva Mills v. Union of India**, the Supreme Court of India held that the power of judicial review is part of the basic structure of the Constitution and cannot be taken away by the government. The case involved a challenge to amendments made to the Constitution, which limited the courts' ability to review certain government actions. The court ruled that judicial review is essential for maintaining the balance between the powers of the legislature, the executive, and the judiciary.

This case affirmed the principle that no administrative or regulatory action is beyond the reach of the courts. Judicial review ensures that regulatory agencies act within their legal limits and do not infringe upon the fundamental rights of individuals.

Judicial Review in Administrative Law

In administrative law, judicial review focuses on three main areas:

1. **Ultra Vires**: Whether the agency acted beyond the scope of its authority.

2. **Reasonableness**: Whether the agency's decision was reasonable and based on sufficient evidence.

3. **Procedural Fairness**: Whether the agency followed due process and provided fair hearings.

In **R (on the application of Miller) v. Secretary of State for Exiting the European Union** (2017), the UK Supreme Court exercised judicial review to rule that the government could not trigger Brexit without Parliament's approval. This case highlighted the importance of judicial review in ensuring that administrative actions align with constitutional principles.

The Power and Responsibility of Regulation

Administrative and regulatory law is the lifeblood of modern governance, dictating the rules by which societies function. Through regulation, agencies ensure public safety, fairness, and order in industries ranging from finance to food, from telecommunications to environmental protection. But with power comes responsibility, and the vocabulary of administrative law constantly reminds us that this power must be exercised within the boundaries of law.

The regulatory state is vast and complex, but it is ultimately driven by a single goal: to balance the interests of individuals, businesses, and the public. By mastering the language of administrative law, we understand not just how to navigate these systems but how to hold them accountable.

"True power in governance lies not in the strength of laws, but in their fair and just application. Regulation is not a tool of control, but a pathway to order and justice."

- **Justice V.R. Krishna Iyer**

Exercises and Practical Applications

1. Rulemaking Simulation:

Imagine you are part of a regulatory agency tasked with drafting new rules for data privacy in social media. Create a draft of the proposed regulation, considering procedural fairness, enforcement mechanisms, and the role of public input.

2. Administrative Tribunal Case:

Participate in a mock adjudication process where a company challenges a fine imposed by a regulatory agency for environmental violations. Present arguments from both sides and discuss the tribunal's final decision.

3. Compliance Audit:

Conduct a hypothetical compliance audit for a financial institution. List the regulatory standards the institution must follow and outline potential risks of non-compliance. Create a strategy for ensuring full compliance with financial regulations.

By completing these exercises, you will gain a deeper understanding of how administrative and regulatory law operates in practice, from rulemaking and enforcement to adjudication and judicial review. This will prepare you to navigate the complex world of regulatory compliance and legal accountability.

Chapter 13: Property Law Vocabulary

"Property rights are not just about things; they are about relationships—relationships between people and things, and relationships between people with respect to things."

\- **Justice Felix Frankfurter**

Property as the Anchor of Society

Property is not merely about ownership of land or buildings; it is about control, security, and legacy. From ancient times, the concept of property has been the foundation of power and civilization. Today, property law continues to govern one of the most fundamental aspects of human existence, the relationship between people and the things they own or control. It spans across the realm of physical property like land and houses to intangible rights like intellectual property.

This chapter will explore the critical vocabulary of property law, unraveling the complex terms that define ownership, rights, duties, and liabilities related to property. Through the lens of real-world case studies and precedents from India and around the world, we will deepen our understanding of property law's practical and philosophical dimensions. These terms, **title**, **ownership**, **lease**, **easement**, and more, form the bedrock of legal discourse in property disputes, transactions, and governance.

As we proceed, you will see that the language of property law is more than just jargon; it is the gateway to understanding the rights and duties that shape the very fabric of society.

Title: The Legal Right to Ownership

Title is the legal foundation upon which ownership of property is based. It establishes a person's legal right to control, possess, and dispose of the property. Without clear title, ownership becomes a contentious issue, and disputes can arise over rightful possession and use.

Case Study: Bishan Das v. State of Punjab (1961)

In **Bishan Das v. State of Punjab (1961)**, the Supreme Court of India dealt with the issue of eviction without due process. Bishan Das was evicted from a property that he claimed ownership of based on his title deed. However, the state argued that the property was government-owned. The court ruled in favor of Bishan Das, stating that the eviction was illegal without providing him an opportunity to defend his title. The judgment emphasized that **title** must be protected, and ownership cannot be arbitrarily taken away.

This case reinforces the principle that **title** is more than just a legal document, it is a recognition of one's right to the property, validated through laws and courts. Without a clear title, property rights are vulnerable, and disputes over ownership can easily arise.

The Importance of Clear Title

In property transactions, having a **clear title** is paramount. It ensures that there are no encumbrances, liens, or disputes over the property. The absence of a clear title can lead to long legal battles, as seen in **State of Haryana v. Mukesh Kumar (2011)**, where the issue of adverse possession clouded the clarity of title and led to a protracted dispute over land ownership.

In this case, the Supreme Court of India ruled that the doctrine of **adverse possession** cannot be used as a weapon by encroachers to claim title to government land. It underlined that title must be protected by the rule of law, and adverse possession, while a legal doctrine, must be applied judiciously.

Ownership: The Bundle of Rights

Ownership in property law is described as a "bundle of rights" because it encompasses various aspects, including the right to possess, use, enjoy, and dispose of property. Ownership can be shared, divided, or subject to certain restrictions, depending on the nature of the property and legal agreements.

Case Study: Kalyani (Dead) by L.R.s v. Narayanan (1980)

In **Kalyani v. Narayanan (1980)**, the Supreme Court of India dealt with a family dispute over property ownership. Several heirs claimed rights to a piece of ancestral property, and the court had to determine each person's share. The ruling clarified the concept of **co-ownership** in property law, where multiple individuals hold joint ownership of a property. Each co-owner has equal rights to possess and enjoy the property unless a specific agreement delineates different shares.

This case is significant because it highlights that **ownership** is not always singular. In many cases, multiple individuals or entities may hold simultaneous ownership rights. This can occur in scenarios of joint tenancy, tenancy-in-common, or co-ownership, where property rights are divided among various parties.

Forms of Co-Ownership: Joint Tenancy and Tenancy in Common

Two of the most common forms of co-ownership are **joint tenancy** and **tenancy in common**. In **joint tenancy**, the co-owners have equal shares, and upon the death of one owner, the ownership automatically passes to the surviving owners (right of survivorship).

In **tenancy in common**, each owner holds an individual share, and that share can be sold or passed on through inheritance.

The difference between these forms of ownership has significant legal implications, particularly in inheritance and property disputes. The Indian case of **Mohar Singh v. Devi Charan** (1988) illustrated the impact of these distinctions, where the court examined how property ownership passed upon the death of one of the tenants.

Possession: Control Over Property

While **ownership** refers to the legal right to a property, **possession** refers to the physical control or occupancy of the property. It is possible to possess a property without owning it, such as in the case of tenants. Likewise, one can own a property without being in possession of it, like in the case of landlords.

Case Study: Anathula Sudhakar v. P. Buchi Reddy (2008)

In **Anathula Sudhakar v. P. Buchi Reddy (2008)**, the Supreme Court of India dealt with a dispute over possession versus ownership. The plaintiff had possession of the land but lacked the legal title to claim ownership. The defendant, on the other hand, had legal title but had never been in possession. The court ruled that possession alone is not sufficient to claim ownership unless it is proven that possession has been adverse to the interests of the rightful owner for the statutory period.

This case highlighted the distinction between **possession** and **ownership** and the legal doctrine of **adverse possession**, where continuous and hostile possession over a certain period can confer ownership rights to the possessor.

Adverse Possession: Gaining Ownership Through Possession

Adverse possession is a legal doctrine that allows a person who occupies land without permission to eventually claim ownership if they have possessed the land openly and continuously for a specific period. The **Karnataka Board of Wakf v. Government of India (2004)** case established that adverse possession must be clear, unequivocal, and hostile to the interests of the true owner.

This principle, while controversial, is an important tool in property law for resolving disputes where the legal owner has neglected their rights, and someone else has effectively taken control of the land.

Easements: The Right to Use Another's Property

An **easement** is a legal right granted to a person to use the land of another for a specific purpose. Common easements include the right of way, which allows someone to pass through another's land, or utility easements, which allow access to install and maintain utilities.

Case Study: P.C. Cheriyan v. Mst. Barfi Devi (1980)

In **P.C. Cheriyan v. Mst. Barfi Devi (1980)**, the Supreme Court of India dealt with the issue of an **easement by prescription**, where the plaintiff had been using a pathway through the defendant's land for over 20 years. The defendant challenged the use, claiming no formal easement existed. The court ruled in favor of the plaintiff, establishing that long-term, uninterrupted use of a right of way creates a legal easement, even in the absence of a formal agreement.

This case illustrates the concept of **prescriptive easements**, which are rights that arise from long-term use, and highlights how easements can sometimes be implied through behavior rather than explicit agreements.

Dominant and Servient Tenements

Easements involve two properties: the **dominant tenement**, which benefits from the easement, and the **servient tenement**, which bears the burden of the easement. In **Bhupinder Singh v. Pritam Singh (2009)**, the court clarified that the servient tenement owner must allow reasonable use of the easement by the dominant tenement owner but can place reasonable restrictions to prevent abuse of the easement.

Understanding the rights and limitations associated with easements is crucial, as they can significantly impact property values and usability.

Leasehold and Freehold: Temporary and Permanent Ownership

Property ownership can be broadly categorized into two forms: **freehold** and **leasehold**. In **freehold**, the owner has absolute ownership of the property, including the land, with no time limit. In **leasehold**, the tenant has the right to use the property for a specific period under a lease agreement, but ownership remains with the landlord.

Case Study: State of West Bengal v. S.K. Ghosh (1963)

In **State of West Bengal v. S.K. Ghosh**, the court examined a case where the government had leased land to private individuals. The lease expired, and the state sought to reclaim the land. The Supreme Court ruled in favor of the

state, stating that once the leasehold term ended, the lessee had no further rights to the property, and it reverted to the government.

This case underscores the temporary nature of **leasehold** ownership and the importance of adhering to the terms of a lease. Leaseholders have the right to use the property, but their rights are limited by time and the specific terms agreed upon with the landlord.

Lease Covenants: Rights and Obligations

Leases often include **covenants**, legally binding promises regarding the use of the property. These covenants can impose obligations on both the landlord and the tenant. In the case of **Shanti Devi v. Amal Kumar Banerjee (1981)**, the court ruled that failure to adhere to the terms of a lease covenant could result in forfeiture of the lease, especially in cases where tenants had violated conditions related to property use.

Understanding the legal implications of leasehold agreements, including covenants and renewal rights, is essential for tenants and landlords alike.

Mortgages and Liens: Securing Interests in Property

A **mortgage** is a legal agreement where property is used as collateral for a loan. If the borrower defaults on the loan, the lender has the right to take possession of the property through foreclosure. Similarly, a **lien** gives creditors a legal claim on the property as security for a debt.

Case Study: Kedar Nath v. Sheonarain (1953)

In **Kedar Nath v. Sheonarain**, the Supreme Court of India dealt with the issue of mortgage redemption. The case involved a borrower who sought to redeem his mortgaged property after the loan term expired. The lender refused to release the property, claiming that the redemption period had lapsed. The court ruled in favor of the borrower, emphasizing the borrower's right to redeem the property by repaying the loan amount, even if there was a delay.

This case illustrates the protective nature of **mortgage law** in India, where borrowers retain significant rights to redeem their property, even in cases of delay, provided they act within the statutory redemption period.

Lien: A Legal Claim on Property

A **lien** is a legal right or interest that a creditor has in the debtor's property until the debt is satisfied. In **Bank of Bihar v. State of Bihar (1972)**, the Supreme Court examined a case involving a lien on movable property. The bank had a lien over goods as security for a loan. When the debtor defaulted, the bank seized the goods. The court upheld the bank's right to exercise the lien, noting that it provided legal security to creditors.

Liens can apply to both movable and immovable property, and understanding the rights they confer is essential for navigating financial transactions involving property.

Covenants and Restrictions: Limiting the Use of Property

Covenants are legally binding promises attached to land, often restricting how the land can be used. These restrictions can be part of a deed or a lease and may include conditions about the types of structures allowed or how the land is to be maintained.

Case Study: Tulk v. Moxhay (1848)

In the English case of **Tulk v. Moxhay**, the court dealt with a restrictive covenant attached to land. The owner of the land had sold it with a condition that no building would be constructed on the open space. The purchaser, Moxhay, who was aware of the covenant, attempted to build on the land. The court ruled against Moxhay, stating that the covenant was binding because he had knowledge of it at the time of purchase.

This case established the principle that **restrictive covenants** can run with the land, meaning that they are enforceable against subsequent owners, not just the original parties to the covenant.

Enforcing Covenants

The enforcement of **covenants** can be challenging, particularly when the land changes hands. In **Ram Chandra v. Municipal Corporation of Delhi (1989)**, the court examined a dispute over a restrictive covenant that limited the height of a building. The property owner attempted to violate the restriction, but the court ruled that the covenant was enforceable, preventing any construction that exceeded the agreed-upon height.

Covenants are vital tools in property law, often used by developers and municipalities to maintain the character of neighborhoods or ensure compliance with environmental standards.

Zoning and Land Use: Government Control Over Property

Zoning laws are government-imposed restrictions on how land can be used in certain areas. These laws divide land into zones, such as residential, commercial, or industrial, each with specific rules governing the types of buildings allowed and their uses.

Case Study: K.T. Plantation Pvt. Ltd. v. State of Karnataka (2011)

In **K.T. Plantation Pvt. Ltd. v. State of Karnataka**, the Supreme Court of India dealt with a case challenging the government's power to acquire land under zoning regulations. The government had acquired land from a private company to create public green spaces. The company argued that the acquisition was unfair and arbitrary. The court upheld the government's action, emphasizing that zoning laws serve a public purpose and that the government has the authority to impose restrictions on land use in the interest of the public.

This case highlights how **zoning laws** can impact property ownership and how governments balance private rights with public needs.

Land Use Planning

Land use planning is a crucial aspect of **zoning**. Municipalities and governments use zoning to control urban growth, preserve natural resources, and ensure that communities develop in an organized and sustainable manner. In **Guruvayoor Devaswom Managing Committee v. Rajan (2003)**, the court ruled that land-use restrictions imposed by municipal authorities must be followed by property owners, even if they conflict with private interests.

Zoning regulations may limit what an owner can do with their property, but they are essential for ensuring that urban areas grow in a way that benefits society as a whole.

Navigating the Vocabulary of Property Law

Property law is a complex and ever-evolving field that touches on the core of human existence, our relationship with the land, buildings, and other assets we claim as our own. The vocabulary of property law reflects the intricate balance between individual ownership rights and societal interests. Terms like **title**, **ownership**, **lease**, **easement**, and **zoning** are not just legal jargon; they are the tools through which justice, fairness, and order are maintained in society.

Through the exploration of these terms and their real-world applications, we gain a deeper understanding of how property law shapes the world around us. Whether it is securing your family home, engaging in real estate transactions, or navigating a lease agreement, mastering the language of property law empowers you to protect your interests and contribute to a just society.

"Property is the soul of the legal system, it is where the abstract principles of law meet the tangible realities of life."

- **Justice M.C. Chagla**

Exercises and Practical Applications

1. Mock Title Dispute:

Participate in a mock title dispute where multiple parties claim ownership of the same property. Present evidence of title, possession, and adverse possession to argue your case.

2. Easement Negotiation:

Simulate a negotiation between a landowner and a utility company seeking an easement to install power lines. Draft the terms of the easement, balancing the needs of both parties.

3. Zoning Appeal:

Prepare an appeal to a zoning board challenging a restriction on building height. Present arguments based on property rights, public interest, and zoning regulations.

Through these exercises, you will enhance your understanding of property law vocabulary and its practical application, preparing you for real-world property disputes and transactions.

Chapter 14: Business and Corporate Law Terms

"Corporate law is the law of enterprise. It provides the framework within which businesses operate, and it must balance the interests of shareholders, employees, and the public."

- **Adolf A. Berle**

The Language of Commerce

Business is the engine that drives modern economies, and corporate law is the framework that governs this engine. Whether it's a small startup or a multinational conglomerate, every business exists within the boundaries of legal structures that define how they operate, grow, and resolve disputes. These legal boundaries are not abstract, they are woven into the very fabric of commercial life through a specific vocabulary. Terms like **corporation**, **liability**, **shareholder**, **merger**, and **fiduciary duty** carry the weight of centuries of legal evolution, protecting both business interests and societal values.

This chapter explores the essential terms of business and corporate law, shedding light on the language that shapes boardroom decisions, investment strategies, and legal battles. Through case studies, precedents, and practical examples, we will dive deep into the world of corporate structures, governance, and the legal protections afforded to businesses. These terms form the bedrock of how businesses are created, sustained, and expanded. Understanding this vocabulary is crucial for anyone involved in commerce, whether as a lawyer, entrepreneur, or corporate executive.

Corporation: The Legal Entity

At the heart of corporate law lies the concept of the **corporation**. A corporation is a legal entity separate from its owners, which means it can enter contracts, sue, be sued, own assets, and incur liabilities in its own name. The corporation as an entity is distinct from its shareholders, providing a shield that protects individual owners from personal liability.

Case Study: Salomon v. Salomon & Co. Ltd. (1897)

The landmark case of **Salomon v. Salomon & Co. Ltd. (1897)** in the UK House of Lords established the principle of corporate personality, or the idea that a company is a separate legal entity from its shareholders. Salomon, a leather merchant, formed a corporation and became its major shareholder. When the company went bankrupt, creditors sought to hold Salomon personally liable for the company's debts. The House of Lords ruled that since the company was legally incorporated, it was distinct from Salomon, and therefore, Salomon was not personally liable.

This case laid the foundation for modern corporate law by affirming that once a business is incorporated, it assumes a separate legal existence. This shield of **limited liability** is one of the most critical aspects of forming a corporation, protecting shareholders from personal financial ruin when the company faces legal or financial trouble.

Limited Liability: The Shield for Shareholders

One of the main benefits of forming a corporation is the protection it offers through **limited liability**. Shareholders are only responsible for the company's debts and obligations to the extent of their investment. In the Indian context, this principle was upheld in **Juggi Lal Kamlapat v. CIT (1969)**, where the Supreme Court reiterated that shareholders cannot be held liable for the company's debts, reinforcing the separation between personal and corporate liability.

Shareholders: Owners of the Corporation

Shareholders are the owners of a corporation, and they invest in the company by purchasing shares. Their ownership gives them certain rights, including voting rights, the right to dividends, and the right to a share of the company's assets if it is liquidated. However, shareholders are typically not involved in the day-to-day management of the company; that responsibility falls to the board of directors and executives.

Case Study: Tata Consultancy Services (TCS) and Shareholder Rights

In India, the rights of shareholders were tested in **Tata Consultancy Services v. Cyrus Mistry (2021)**. The case arose when Tata Sons, the holding company of TCS, removed its chairman, Cyrus Mistry, sparking a bitter legal battle. Mistry, a minority shareholder, challenged his removal, citing governance failures and mismanagement by the majority shareholders. The National Company Law Tribunal (NCLT) ruled in favor of Tata Sons, stating that Mistry's removal was within the company's legal rights. However, the case brought to light the tension between **majority** and **minority shareholders** and the rights of each under Indian corporate law.

This case demonstrated how corporate law balances the interests of **majority shareholders** (who often control the company) and **minority shareholders** (who have limited power but still hold significant rights). In large corporations, these dynamics can lead to disputes over control, governance, and accountability.

Fiduciary Duty: The Obligation of Trust

At the core of corporate governance lies the concept of **fiduciary duty**. Directors and officers of a company are fiduciaries, they are entrusted with the responsibility of acting in the best interests of the company and its shareholders. This duty includes the duty of loyalty, the duty of care, and the duty to act in good faith.

Case Study: Satyam Scandal (2009)

The infamous **Satyam Scandal** in India brought to light the catastrophic consequences of breaching fiduciary duties. Ramalinga Raju, the founder and CEO of Satyam Computer Services, confessed to falsifying the company's financial statements over several years, inflating the company's assets and profits. This resulted in billions of dollars in losses to shareholders and irreparable damage to the company's reputation. Raju's actions were a clear violation of his **fiduciary duty** to act in the best interests of the company and its shareholders.

The case led to widespread reforms in corporate governance, including stricter regulations on corporate transparency and accountability through the **Companies Act, 2013**. The scandal demonstrated how breaches of fiduciary duty can destroy a corporation and harm thousands of investors.

Duty of Loyalty and Duty of Care

Duty of loyalty means that directors must put the company's interests ahead of their own, avoiding conflicts of interest. **Duty of care** requires that directors make informed decisions, acting with the care that a reasonably prudent person would exercise in a similar situation. In the **Smith v. Van Gorkom (1985)** case, the Delaware Supreme Court held that the board of Trans Union Corporation had breached its duty of care by approving a merger without sufficient information, illustrating the importance of diligence in corporate decision-making.

Corporate Governance: The Framework of Accountability

Corporate governance refers to the system of rules, practices, and processes by which a company is directed and controlled. Good corporate governance ensures that the company operates transparently, ethically, and in compliance with the law, while safeguarding the interests of shareholders, employees, and the public.

Case Study: Infosys and Corporate Governance

Infosys, one of India's largest IT companies, has long been seen as a model of **corporate governance**. However, in 2017, the company faced internal turmoil when its co-founder, Narayana Murthy, raised concerns about governance failures, including executive compensation and the handling of acquisitions. The board's handling of these issues led to the resignation of the then-CEO, Vishal Sikka. Though the company survived the crisis, it highlighted the delicate balance between board authority and shareholder concerns, as well as the importance of transparency in corporate governance.

This incident underscores that corporate governance is not just about compliance with legal norms but also about building trust among stakeholders. The principles of accountability, fairness, and transparency are central to maintaining a company's reputation and long-term success.

Board of Directors: Decision-Makers of the Corporation

The **board of directors** is responsible for overseeing the management of the corporation. Directors are tasked with making strategic decisions and ensuring that the company complies with the law. However, directors are not immune from liability if they act negligently or breach their fiduciary duties. In the case of **Delhi Development Authority v. Skipper Construction Co. (1996)**, the Supreme Court of India held the directors personally liable for fraudulent activities conducted by the company, highlighting the limits of the **corporate veil** and ensuring that directors cannot hide behind their positions to escape responsibility.

Merger and Acquisition: Combining Corporate Entities

A **merger** occurs when two companies combine to form a single entity, while an **acquisition** involves one company purchasing another. These transactions are often motivated by the desire to expand market share, increase efficiency, or gain a competitive advantage.

Case Study: Vodafone-Idea Merger (2018)

In 2018, two of India's largest telecom companies, Vodafone India and Idea Cellular, merged to create **Vodafone Idea Ltd.**, one of the largest telecom operators in the country. The merger was driven by the intense competition in the telecom sector, particularly with the entry of Reliance Jio, which disrupted the market with its low-cost data plans. The merger allowed Vodafone and Idea to pool their resources, reduce costs, and remain competitive.

This case illustrates the strategic use of **mergers** to survive in highly competitive industries. However, mergers and acquisitions often come with regulatory hurdles. In the Vodafone-Idea case, the merger had to be approved by the **Competition Commission of India (CCI)** to ensure that it did not create a monopoly or reduce competition in the market.

Takeovers and Hostile Acquisitions

A **hostile takeover** occurs when a company is acquired against the wishes of its board of directors. This often happens through the purchase of a majority of the company's shares on the open market. In the case of **Tata Tea v. SEC of India (2001)**, the Securities and Exchange Board of

India (SEBI) intervened to prevent Tata Tea from being taken over in a hostile bid by a foreign competitor. SEBI's regulations ensure that takeovers are conducted fairly, with protections in place for minority shareholders.

Mergers and acquisitions are powerful tools for corporate expansion, but they require careful navigation of regulatory landscapes and consideration of the rights of all stakeholders involved.

Corporate Liability: Holding Companies Accountable

While corporations provide limited liability for their shareholders, they are not immune from being held liable for their own actions. **Corporate liability** extends to breaches of law, environmental damage, and even criminal conduct.

Case Study: Union Carbide and the Bhopal Gas Tragedy (1984)

The **Bhopal Gas Tragedy** remains one of the most catastrophic examples of corporate liability in history. In 1984, a gas leak from a Union Carbide pesticide plant in Bhopal, India, killed thousands of people and left countless others with severe health problems. Union

Carbide was held liable for the disaster, and after years of litigation, the company paid $470 million in compensation to the victims.

This case demonstrates the importance of **corporate responsibility** and the need for companies to adhere to safety standards and ethical practices. The principle of corporate liability ensures that companies can be held accountable for the harm they cause, even when the harm extends far beyond financial loss.

Criminal Liability of Corporations

Corporations can also be held **criminally liable** for actions such as fraud, bribery, and environmental violations. In **Standard Chartered Bank v. Directorate of Enforcement (2005)**, the Supreme Court of India ruled that a corporation can be held criminally liable and fined for regulatory violations, even if imprisonment is not possible for corporate entities. This case clarified that corporate entities are not immune from criminal law and can face significant penalties for misconduct.

Contracts in Business Law: The Legal Framework of Deals

Contracts are the backbone of business transactions, ensuring that agreements are enforceable by law. A contract is a legally binding agreement between two or more parties, and it can cover anything from the sale of goods to complex service agreements.

Case Study: Balfour v. Balfour (1919)

In the English case of **Balfour v. Balfour (1919)**, the court examined the issue of intention in contract formation. A husband promised to pay his wife an allowance while he worked abroad, but when the relationship soured, the wife sued for the unpaid allowance. The court ruled that agreements made in a domestic context are not typically intended to be legally binding. This case emphasized the importance of **intention to create legal relations**, which is a key element in contract law.

Contracts are a foundational element of business law, and understanding the terms of a contract is essential for avoiding disputes. In business settings, contracts ensure that parties meet their obligations and that there are legal remedies available if they do not.

Breach of Contract and Remedies

A **breach of contract** occurs when one party fails to fulfill their contractual obligations. In **Hadley v. Baxendale (1854)**, the court established the principle of **remoteness of damages**, stating that damages for breach of contract are limited to losses that are reasonably foreseeable. This principle is critical in assessing how much compensation a party can claim for a breach.

Contracts provide the structure for business operations, but when disputes arise, understanding remedies such as **specific performance**, **damages**, and **rescission** is essential for resolving conflicts.

Corporate Social Responsibility (CSR): Balancing Profit with Purpose

In recent years, **Corporate Social Responsibility (CSR)** has become a significant part of corporate governance. CSR refers to the idea that businesses have a responsibility not just to their shareholders, but also to society at large. Companies are now expected to contribute to social causes, protect the environment, and ensure ethical practices in their operations.

Case Study: Reliance Industries' CSR Initiatives

Reliance Industries, one of India's largest conglomerates, has been at the forefront of CSR in India. Through the Reliance Foundation, the company has invested in education, healthcare, and rural development. This approach aligns with the **Companies Act, 2013**, which mandates that large companies spend at least 2% of their average net profit on CSR activities.

CSR is not just about philanthropy; it is about integrating social and environmental concerns into a company's business operations. Companies that embrace CSR are often seen as more ethical and sustainable, which can enhance their reputation and brand value.

Legal Mandates for CSR

India is one of the few countries that legally mandates CSR. Under Section 135 of the **Companies Act, 2013**, companies meeting certain thresholds must allocate a percentage of their profits to CSR activities. This legal mandate ensures that businesses contribute to societal welfare, promoting sustainability and ethical practices.

The Heart of Business Law

Business and corporate law is not just a set of rules; it is the framework that makes commerce possible. From the protection of shareholder rights to the accountability of directors, from the formation of contracts to the consequences of breaches, corporate law provides the stability and trust upon which businesses operate. It defines the boundaries of ethical conduct, ensures the accountability of corporations, and balances the competing interests of shareholders, employees, and society at large.

The vocabulary of corporate law is more than technical jargon, it is the language of trust, governance, and justice. By mastering these terms and understanding their practical implications, we gain the tools to navigate the complex world of business with confidence and integrity.

"In the end, corporate law is about building a foundation where trust can thrive, where businesses can grow responsibly, and where justice can prevail even in the most complex of commercial disputes."

- **Justice B.N. Kirpal**

Exercises and Practical Applications

1. Mock Corporate Merger:

Participate in a mock corporate merger between two companies. Draft the merger agreement, focusing on shareholder rights, fiduciary duties, and regulatory approvals.

2. Fiduciary Duty Scenario:

Simulate a board of directors meeting where a conflict of interest arises. Discuss how fiduciary duties of loyalty and care should guide the board's decision-making process.

3. Contract Breach Analysis:

Analyze a breach of contract case involving a failed business agreement. Identify the remedies available to the injured party and argue for the appropriate compensation based on contract law principles.

These exercises will help you apply the vocabulary and concepts of business and corporate law, preparing you for real-world commercial transactions and legal challenges.

Chapter 15: Criminal Law Terminology

"Justice, though it may sometimes be delayed, always demands that wrongs be acknowledged, that truth prevails, and that those who have caused harm face the consequences of their actions."

\- **Justice H.R. Khanna**

Understanding the Language of Crime and Punishment

Criminal law is the force that upholds societal order. It sets the boundaries of acceptable behavior, ensures justice for victims, and defines the punishment for wrongdoers. But at the heart of this system is a language, specific terminology that transforms concepts like guilt, innocence, and punishment into actionable legal rules. This vocabulary is not just a tool for lawyers and judges; it's the very framework through which society deals with crime and its aftermath.

Terms such as **mens rea**, **actus reus**, **indictment**, **arraignment**, **felony**, and **misdemeanor** are more than technicalities; they are the cornerstones of how criminal justice functions. Each term carries with it centuries of legal development, societal values, and judicial interpretation. This chapter will explore these foundational terms, along with relevant case law, to provide a clear understanding of the language that shapes criminal law.

Through powerful real-life case studies, we will unravel the meanings behind these terms, exploring their practical application in courtrooms, and their profound significance in delivering justice. By the end of this chapter, you will not only know these terms but also appreciate the human stories, ethical dilemmas, and legal battles they represent.

Mens Rea: The Guilty Mind

At the core of most crimes is the concept of **mens rea**, meaning "guilty mind" in Latin. Mens rea refers to the mental state of the accused at the time of committing the offense. It distinguishes between those who act with intent and those whose actions are accidental.

Case Study: R v. Cunningham (1957)

In **R v. Cunningham (1957)**, the defendant tore a gas meter off the wall to steal money, causing a gas leak that endangered the lives of nearby residents. The court had to determine whether Cunningham acted with **mens rea**, that is, whether he intended to cause harm or was reckless as to the consequences of his actions. The court ruled that **recklessness** was sufficient to establish mens rea in this case. Cunningham may not have intended the specific harm, but his reckless disregard for the potential consequences made him criminally liable.

This case highlights how **mens rea** can take different forms, including intention, recklessness, and negligence. Criminal liability often hinges on proving the mental state of the accused at the time of the offense, as it reflects their culpability.

Intention vs. Recklessness

In criminal law, the distinction between **intention** and **recklessness** is crucial. **Intention** refers to a deliberate and purposeful action, while **recklessness** involves taking an unjustifiable risk. The Indian case of **Santokh Singh v. Izhar Hussain (1973)** demonstrated this distinction when the Supreme Court had to decide if the defendant, by firing a gun in a crowded space, had intended to kill or acted recklessly. The court ruled that firing the weapon in such circumstances demonstrated recklessness, making him culpable under the law.

Actus Reus: The Guilty Act

While **mens rea** focuses on the defendant's state of mind, **actus reus** refers to the physical act of the crime. A criminal offense typically requires both a guilty mind and a guilty act. The law punishes not just thoughts but the actions that translate those thoughts into reality.

Case Study: State of Maharashtra v. Mohd. Yakub (1980)

In **State of Maharashtra v. Mohd. Yakub**, the Supreme Court of India examined whether preparations for committing an offense could amount to **actus reus**. The defendant was caught preparing to smuggle goods, and while the actual act had not been committed, the court ruled that his actions constituted an attempt, a criminal offense in itself. This case illustrates how the law interprets **attempts** as part of the **actus reus**, recognizing that even incomplete actions can be criminally liable.

This case emphasizes the principle that the physical act of crime does not always have to result in harm; the very act of attempting a crime, when coupled with the intent, is punishable.

Omissions as Actus Reus

Criminal liability can also arise from **omissions**, failing to act when there is a legal duty to do so. In **Gibbons v. Proctor (1918)**, a stepfather who failed to feed his child was found guilty of murder through omission. He had a legal duty to care for the child, and his failure to act resulted in death. In such cases, the **actus reus** is not an action but the failure to perform a required duty.

Indictment and Arraignment: The Road to Trial

The terms **indictment** and **arraignment** mark critical stages in the criminal process, ensuring that the accused is formally charged and given an opportunity to respond to the charges.

Case Study: The Indictment in State v. Sanjay Dutt (1993)

The high-profile case of **State v. Sanjay Dutt**, connected to the 1993 Mumbai bomb blasts, offers a clear illustration of **indictment**. Dutt was indicted under the **Terrorist and Disruptive Activities (Prevention) Act (TADA)** for possession of illegal arms. The indictment laid out the formal charges against him, setting the stage for his trial. The case demonstrates the seriousness of formal charges and the role of the indictment in framing the specific accusations the defendant must defend against in court.

Arraignment and Plea

Once indicted, the accused must go through **arraignment**, a formal court proceeding where they are informed of the charges and asked to enter a plea, guilty or not guilty. The importance of arraignment was highlighted in **United States v. Marion (1971)**, where the U.S. Supreme Court emphasized that the right to a speedy trial begins at the time of indictment or arraignment. In India, the procedure is governed by Section 228 of the **Criminal Procedure Code (CrPC)**, ensuring that the accused is aware of the charges and can prepare a defense.

Felony and Misdemeanor: Classifying Crimes

Crimes are often classified based on their severity into **felonies** and **misdemeanors**. Understanding the difference between these two classifications helps in determining the gravity of the offense, the procedures to follow, and the possible punishments.

Case Study: Indian Penal Code and Felony Classifications

Under the **Indian Penal Code (IPC)**, serious offenses like murder, rape, and robbery are classified as felonies, punishable by long-term imprisonment or even death. For example, in **Maqbool Hussain v. State of Bombay (1953)**, the Supreme Court of India dealt with the issue of double jeopardy, where a person was punished under the **Sea Customs Act** but then tried again under the IPC for smuggling gold, a felony. The case highlighted how felonies are treated with utmost seriousness, often involving severe penalties.

In contrast, lesser offenses such as petty theft or minor assaults are considered misdemeanors and carry lighter sentences, often involving fines or short-term imprisonment. The differentiation between **felony** and **misdemeanor** is critical for determining the applicable legal procedures and consequences.

Misdemeanors and Proportional Punishment

Misdemeanors, though less severe, still demand accountability. In the U.S. case of **Robinson v. California (1962)**, the U.S. Supreme Court ruled that punishing a person for a status offense, such as drug addiction, was unconstitutional. The case drew a distinction between criminal acts and conditions, emphasizing that punishment must be proportional to the crime. This principle is mirrored in Indian law, where lesser offenses are treated with a proportional approach to sentencing, ensuring fairness in the justice system.

Defenses to Criminal Liability: Navigating the Complexities of Justification

Criminal law recognizes that not every action that results in harm is necessarily criminal. Certain defenses, such as **insanity**, **self-**

defense, and **duress**, can absolve an individual of criminal liability if proven.

Case Study: Self-Defense in the Vishwanath v. State of Uttar Pradesh (1960)

In **Vishwanath v. State of Uttar Pradesh**, the defendant claimed self-defense after killing a man who attacked him with a knife. The Supreme Court ruled that the right to **self-defense** allows a person to protect themselves from imminent harm, even if it results in the death of the attacker, provided the force used is proportional to the threat.

This case underscores the significance of **justification defenses** in criminal law. Self-defense is not just about preserving one's life; it reflects the principle that the law recognizes the right to protect oneself from unlawful aggression.

Insanity as a Defense

The **insanity defense** operates on the principle that a person who lacks the capacity to understand the nature of their actions or distinguish between right and wrong should not be held criminally responsible. The case of **McNaghten's Case (1843)** in England established the **McNaghten Rule**, which became the standard for determining criminal insanity. Under this rule, a defendant must prove that, at the time of the crime, they were suffering from a mental disorder that rendered them incapable of understanding their actions.

Indian courts have also recognized the insanity defense, as seen in **State of Rajasthan v. Shera Ram (2011)**, where the Supreme Court ruled in favor of the defendant, who had a long history of mental illness. The court acquitted him on grounds of insanity, illustrating how mental health conditions intersect with criminal liability.

Criminal Procedure: The Path from Arrest to Conviction

Criminal law is not just about punishing wrongdoers; it is about ensuring that justice is carried out through a fair and lawful process. The steps from **arrest** to **conviction** are governed by strict procedures that protect the rights of both the accused and society.

Arrest and Detention: Legal Limits

The process of arrest must follow legal protocols, ensuring that the rights of the accused are respected. In **D.K. Basu v. State of West Bengal (1997)**, the Supreme Court of India laid down specific guidelines for arrest and detention to prevent custodial abuse. The court ruled that every person arrested must be informed of the reasons for their arrest and their right to consult a lawyer, among other safeguards.

This landmark ruling reinforced the idea that while the state has the power to arrest and detain individuals suspected of committing crimes, it must exercise this power within the confines of the law, respecting fundamental rights.

Bail: The Right to Temporary Freedom

Once arrested, the accused may apply for **bail**, which allows them to remain free until their trial. The grant of bail depends on the severity of the offense, the risk of flight, and the likelihood of tampering with evidence. In **Moti Ram v. State of Madhya Pradesh (1978)**, the Supreme Court stressed the importance of the right to bail, particularly for poor and marginalized individuals. The court held that bail should not be denied on the grounds of poverty, and that excessive bail amounts violate constitutional rights.

Bail ensures a balance between individual liberty and the state's interest in prosecuting offenders. It is a critical component of the criminal justice process, ensuring that the accused is not unjustly deprived of freedom before a conviction is secured.

Sentencing and Punishment: The Consequences of Guilt

Once a person is convicted of a crime, the next stage is sentencing, where the court decides the appropriate punishment. Sentencing can range from fines and community service to imprisonment and even the death penalty, depending on the severity of the crime and the circumstances surrounding it.

Case Study: Bachan Singh v. State of Punjab (1980)

In **Bachan Singh v. State of Punjab**, the Supreme Court of India addressed the issue of capital punishment. The court upheld the constitutionality of the **death penalty**, but only in the "rarest of rare" cases, where the crime was so heinous that no other punishment would suffice. The judgment introduced the principle of proportionality in sentencing, ensuring that the punishment fits the crime while also considering mitigating factors.

This case is a powerful reminder of the gravity of criminal sentencing, especially in cases involving the death penalty. It also reflects the moral and legal challenges that arise when determining the appropriate punishment for serious offenses.

The Role of Mitigating and Aggravating Factors

In sentencing, courts must consider **mitigating** and **aggravating factors**. Mitigating factors, such as the defendant's age, mental health, or lack of prior criminal record, can lead to a reduced sentence. Aggravating factors, such as the use of extreme violence or the targeting of vulnerable victims, can result in harsher penalties. In **State of Kerala v. Rajesh (2020)**, the Supreme Court highlighted the importance of carefully weighing these factors to ensure that justice is served.

Conclusion: The Vocabulary of Crime and Justice

Criminal law is not just a set of rules; it is a complex system that reflects society's values, balances rights and duties, and ensures justice. The terminology of criminal law, **mens rea**, **actus reus**, **indictment**, **self-defense**, and **sentencing**, is more than legal jargon. It is the language that defines how we deal with wrongdoing, hold individuals accountable, and protect the innocent.

Understanding these terms is not merely about knowing definitions; it is about appreciating the human stories, moral dilemmas, and legal principles that underpin the criminal justice system. Through the exploration of real-life cases and legal precedents, we gain a deeper insight into the functioning of criminal law and the immense responsibility it carries in shaping a just society.

"Crime is not just an act against the state, but a breach of the social contract that binds us together. Justice, therefore, is not just a matter of law but a fulfillment of our collective responsibility to uphold fairness, truth, and humanity."

\- **Justice Y.V. Chandrachud**

Exercises and Practical Applications

1. Mock Trial:

Participate in a mock criminal trial where you represent either the prosecution or the defense. Present evidence, argue about **mens rea** and **actus reus**, and make a closing statement about the appropriate sentence.

2. Sentencing Debate:

Analyze a high-profile criminal case and debate whether the sentence handed down was just. Discuss the role of mitigating and aggravating factors in the court's decision.

3. Defenses in Criminal Law:

Choose a real-life criminal case and evaluate whether a defense such as **insanity** or **self-defense** would have been applicable. Present arguments for both sides.

By completing these exercises, you will deepen your understanding of criminal law terminology and its practical implications, preparing you for real-world legal scenarios.

Chapter 16: Criminal Procedure Vocabulary

"The foundation of justice lies not in punishment, but in the process that ensures fairness, equality, and the rule of law for all."

\- **Justice H.R. Khanna**

The Path to Justice Through Procedure

In the realm of criminal law, the importance of **procedure** cannot be overstated. Procedure is the vehicle through which justice is delivered. It is the process that ensures every individual, regardless of their status, is treated fairly and in accordance with the law. While criminal law defines offenses and their punishments, criminal procedure defines **how** those laws are applied. The vocabulary of criminal procedure, though technical, is essential in safeguarding the rights of the accused and ensuring that the truth is revealed in the most just way possible.

This chapter will explore the critical terms in criminal procedure, **arrest**, **bail**, **charge sheet**, **summons**, and **warrant**, and provide real-world case studies to illustrate their application. We will dive into the complexities of each stage, from the moment a crime is reported to the final appeal, showing how these legal steps shape the path to justice.

The language of criminal procedure is not just about adhering to rules; it is about protecting human dignity, ensuring accountability, and upholding the rule of law. As we walk through these terms, we will uncover how they influence the course of justice in ways both subtle and profound.

Arrest: The First Step in Criminal Procedure

An **arrest** is the first tangible step in the criminal justice process. It is the act of taking a person into custody, usually because they are suspected of committing a crime. However, an arrest is not merely a physical act, it is a legal one, bounded by laws that protect the individual's rights.

Case Study: D.K. Basu v. State of West Bengal (1997)

In the landmark case of **D.K. Basu v. State of West Bengal (1997)**, the Supreme Court of India set forth guidelines to prevent custodial violence and ensure that arrests are carried out with due regard for human dignity. D.K. Basu, a human rights activist, filed a petition highlighting cases of custodial deaths in police stations. The court ruled that any person arrested must be informed of the grounds for their arrest, be allowed to consult with a lawyer, and have their arrest documented.

This case established the critical balance between the state's power to arrest and the individual's fundamental rights. The guidelines set forth by the court emphasize that the power to arrest is not absolute. Law enforcement must adhere to due process, ensuring that the rights of the accused are not violated.

Legal Requirements for Arrest

In India, the **Criminal Procedure Code (CrPC)** outlines the procedures for arrest. According to Section 41 of the CrPC, police officers can arrest without a warrant if they suspect a cognizable offense has been committed. However, the **arrest** must be based on reasonable suspicion, and unnecessary arrests are discouraged. The Supreme Court, in the case of **Arnesh Kumar v. State of Bihar (2014)**, further reinforced this by mandating that arrests for offenses with a punishment of fewer than seven years should not be made automatically, without a thorough assessment of the necessity.

This principle underscores that arrest is a critical step but should be used judiciously, ensuring that the liberty of individuals is not curtailed unnecessarily.

Bail: The Right to Temporary Freedom

Bail is a fundamental part of criminal procedure, ensuring that a person accused of a crime can remain free while awaiting trial. It reflects the principle that an accused person is innocent until proven guilty and that they should not be deprived of their liberty unless absolutely necessary.

Case Study: Moti Ram v. State of Madhya Pradesh (1978)

The Supreme Court's judgment in **Moti Ram v. State of Madhya Pradesh (1978)** is a defining case in the understanding of bail in India. Moti Ram, a poor mason, was granted bail, but the conditions set by the court required him to furnish surety of an amount that he could not afford. The court, realizing the injustice of setting unaffordable bail amounts, ruled that bail conditions must take into account the financial capability of the accused. The ruling stressed that poverty should not prevent a person from securing their freedom.

This case highlights a key aspect of the **right to bail**, that bail should not be punitive. Instead, it should reflect a balance between ensuring the accused appears in court and respecting their right to freedom.

Types of Bail

Bail can take different forms, depending on the nature of the offense. **Regular bail** is granted under Section 437 of the CrPC when an individual is in custody, while **anticipatory bail** (Section 438 of the CrPC) is sought when a person fears arrest. **Interim bail** is granted temporarily, pending the final decision on regular bail.

The **Siddharam Satlingappa Mhetre v. State of Maharashtra (2010)** case dealt with anticipatory bail, where the Supreme Court ruled that it could be granted to protect the liberty of individuals, especially in cases where arrest may be used as a form of harassment. This case reiterated the role of bail in protecting personal freedom and preventing the misuse of arrest powers.

Charge Sheet: Formalizing the Accusation

A **charge sheet** is the document that formally lays out the charges against the accused after an investigation has been completed. It is filed by the police and signals the beginning of the trial process, bringing clarity to the accusations.

Case Study: Suresh Jindal v. State of Delhi (2001)

In the **Suresh Jindal v. State of Delhi (2001)** case, the accused challenged the validity of the charge sheet filed against him, arguing that the police had not conducted a thorough investigation. The court ruled that while the charge sheet is a critical document in the criminal process, it is not the final word. The court retains the discretion to discharge the accused if the evidence is insufficient.

This case illustrates the procedural importance of a charge sheet in framing the charges but also reminds us that the court has the final say in whether the charges should lead to a trial.

Filing and Contents of the Charge Sheet

According to Section 173 of the CrPC, the **charge sheet** must be filed after the investigation is complete. It contains details of the evidence collected, the statements of witnesses, and the specific charges against the accused. The police must present a charge sheet within 90 days of arrest for serious offenses, as per the **CrPC**, or the accused becomes eligible for bail. This timeline reflects the need for efficiency in the criminal justice process, ensuring that the accused does not languish in custody indefinitely.

The charge sheet is essential in crystallizing the accusations and providing the accused with a clear understanding of the case they must defend against.

Summons and Warrants: The Authority to Compel Appearance

Summons and **warrants** are tools the court uses to compel the appearance of the accused or witnesses in court. They ensure that those involved in a legal case are present when required and that the process can move forward without unnecessary delays.

Case Study: Hardeep Singh v. State of Punjab (2014)

In **Hardeep Singh v. State of Punjab (2014)**, the Supreme Court dealt with the issue of summoning additional accused during the trial. The court ruled that if new evidence comes to light, the court has the authority to issue summons to those not originally charged. This case is a reminder of the dynamic nature of criminal trials, where new evidence can reshape the case, necessitating additional summons.

Summons vs. Warrant

A **summons** is a legal document that requests a person to appear in court. It is generally used when there is no immediate need for arrest or when the person is not a flight risk. On the other hand, a **warrant** is issued when the court believes that the individual may not comply with a summons or when the severity of the offense warrants immediate arrest.

In **State of Uttar Pradesh v. Poosu (1976)**, the Supreme Court emphasized that warrants should not be issued lightly. They should only be used when necessary, ensuring that an individual's liberty is not unduly interfered with. This case established the principle that the state must carefully weigh the decision to issue a warrant, balancing the need for compliance with respect for personal freedom.

Cognizable and Non-Cognizable Offenses: The Power to Arrest Without a Warrant

Crimes are classified into **cognizable** and **non-cognizable** offenses, based on the power of the police to arrest without a warrant. Understanding this distinction is critical, as it affects the immediacy of law enforcement action.

Case Study: Lalita Kumari v. Govt. of Uttar Pradesh (2014)

The case of **Lalita Kumari v. Govt. of Uttar Pradesh (2014)** dealt with the mandatory registration of FIRs for **cognizable offenses**. Lalita Kumari had reported a kidnapping, but the police refused to register the FIR, citing a lack of preliminary investigation. The Supreme Court ruled that for cognizable offenses, the police must register an FIR immediately, as delays can hinder justice.

This case clarified the importance of timely police action in cognizable cases, where immediate intervention is necessary to protect public safety or prevent further harm.

Cognizable vs. Non-Cognizable Offenses

In **cognizable offenses**, such as murder, robbery, or

rape, the police have the authority to arrest without a warrant and begin an investigation immediately. **Non-cognizable offenses**, like defamation or public nuisance, require a warrant for arrest, and the police cannot begin an investigation without a magistrate's approval.

The distinction between these categories reflects the severity of the offense and the urgency required in responding to it. Cognizable offenses demand swift action, while non-cognizable offenses follow a more measured legal process.

First Information Report (FIR): Initiating the Criminal Process

The **First Information Report (FIR)** is the document that officially records a complaint about a cognizable offense. It marks the beginning of the criminal investigation process and sets the wheels of justice in motion.

Case Study: Priyanka Srivastava v. State of Uttar Pradesh (2015)

In **Priyanka Srivastava v. State of Uttar Pradesh (2015)**, the Supreme Court emphasized that false or frivolous FIRs must be discouraged. The court ruled that while the police must register FIRs for cognizable offenses, there must also be safeguards to prevent the abuse of this process. This case highlighted the balance between ensuring access to justice and preventing the misuse of legal procedures.

Importance of the FIR

An **FIR** is crucial as it initiates the police investigation. It must contain the details of the offense, the time and place of the occurrence, and the identity of the accused (if known). The filing of an FIR sets in motion the legal obligations of the police to investigate and gather evidence. It is an essential part of ensuring that the criminal process begins in a structured and legally compliant manner.

Trial and Evidence: The Quest for Truth

The **trial** is the heart of the criminal procedure, where evidence is presented, witnesses are examined, and arguments are made. The goal of the trial is to ascertain the truth and deliver justice through a fair process.

Case Study: State of Maharashtra v. Suresh (2000)

In **State of Maharashtra v. Suresh (2000)**, the Supreme Court of India reiterated the importance of a fair trial, stating that the accused must be given every opportunity to present their case, and the evidence must be weighed impartially. In this case, the accused's conviction was overturned due to procedural irregularities that violated his right to a fair trial. The court emphasized that **due process** is the foundation of criminal justice, and no conviction should stand if the trial was compromised.

Burden of Proof and Standards of Evidence

In criminal trials, the **burden of proof** lies with the prosecution, which must prove the accused's guilt "beyond a reasonable doubt." This standard is the highest in the legal system, reflecting the severity of criminal punishment. If the prosecution fails to meet this standard, the accused is entitled to acquittal.

The **Supreme Court of India**, in **Narendra Singh v. State of M.P. (2004)**, ruled that evidence must be credible and reliable. In cases where doubt remains, the benefit of that doubt must be given to the accused. This principle safeguards against wrongful convictions, ensuring that justice is not only served but also seen to be fair.

Appeal: The Final Review

An **appeal** is the process of seeking a higher court's review of a lower court's decision. It ensures that any errors made during the trial can be corrected, and that justice is ultimately upheld.

Case Study: Nirbhaya Rape Case (2012)

The **Nirbhaya Rape Case (2012)**, one of the most horrific crimes in recent Indian history, saw multiple appeals in the higher courts. After the trial court convicted the accused and sentenced them to death, the case went through several layers of judicial review, including the **Delhi High Court** and the **Supreme Court of India**. The appeals focused on procedural fairness, the admissibility of evidence, and the proportionality of the death sentence.

The appeals process in this case demonstrated the importance of judicial review in ensuring that the punishment fits the crime and that every legal avenue is explored before the final judgment is rendered.

Right to Appeal

The right to **appeal** is a fundamental part of criminal procedure. Both the accused and the prosecution have the right to appeal a decision they believe is unjust or erroneous. The **Supreme Court** has held in **Tukaram v. State of Maharashtra (1979)** that every individual has the right to challenge their conviction and seek justice from higher courts, reinforcing the principle that justice must be thorough and comprehensive.

The Vocabulary of Justice in Action

Criminal procedure is the framework through which justice is pursued, ensuring that the accused are treated fairly, the truth is uncovered, and society is protected. Every term in criminal procedure, from **arrest** to **appeal**, carries immense weight, influencing the course of justice and the protection of individual rights.

The cases and principles we have explored demonstrate that while criminal law punishes wrongdoing, criminal procedure ensures that the path to punishment is paved with fairness, due process, and respect for human dignity. Without the precise and careful application of criminal procedure, justice cannot be served.

"In the quest for justice, it is not the outcome that matters most, but the process that we follow to reach that outcome. Only through fair procedure can we ensure true justice."

- Justice P.N. Bhagwati

Exercises and Practical Applications

1. Mock Bail Hearing:

Participate in a mock bail hearing where you represent either the prosecution or the defense. Argue whether bail should be granted, considering the seriousness of the offense and the risk of flight.

2. Draft a Charge Sheet:

Draft a charge sheet based on a hypothetical criminal case, including all necessary details such as the charges, evidence, and witness statements.

3. FIR Analysis:

Analyze a real FIR from a recent case. Discuss whether it meets the legal requirements and how it influences the subsequent investigation.

These exercises will help you apply the vocabulary and principles of criminal procedure, deepening your understanding of how justice is pursued in real-world legal scenarios.

Chapter 17: Mastering Legal Writing Vocabulary

"The language of the law must be clear, precise, and persuasive. It must leave no room for ambiguity or misinterpretation."

- **Justice Louis Brandeis**

The Power of Legal Writing

Legal writing is the craft of clarity and precision. In law, every word carries weight, every phrase must be exact, and every sentence must build toward a purpose. Legal documents, whether they are contracts, briefs, opinions, or pleadings, have a unique structure and language that set them apart from other forms of writing. This specialized vocabulary reflects the centuries-old tradition of law, yet it is also the modern tool through which justice is served.

This chapter explores the essential vocabulary of legal writing, guiding you through terms like **brief**, **memorandum**, **motion**, **opinion**, and **pleading**. Through case studies and examples, we will analyze the power of legal language in influencing decisions, shaping arguments, and ensuring fairness. The goal is to not only familiarize you with these terms but also help you master their practical application in legal documents.

Legal writing is more than a technical skill, it is an art. It requires clarity, precision, and the ability to communicate complex ideas in the simplest, most effective way. Whether you are drafting a contract or arguing in court, mastering legal writing vocabulary will be key to your success.

Brief: A Tool of Persuasion

The **legal brief** is one of the most fundamental documents in litigation. It is a written argument submitted to a court that outlines the legal reasons why one party should prevail. A brief presents the facts, laws, and precedents in a structured and persuasive manner, guiding the court to a conclusion favorable to the submitting party.

Case Study: Kesavananda Bharati v. State of Kerala (1973)

In the landmark case of **Kesavananda Bharati v. State of Kerala**, the Supreme Court of India examined the constitutional limits of parliamentary power. The briefs submitted by both sides were crucial in shaping the court's understanding of the issues. The petitioners argued that the Parliament's power to amend the Constitution was not unlimited and could not destroy the "basic structure" of the Constitution. The government, on the other hand, argued that Parliament's power to amend was absolute.

The briefs in this case played a pivotal role in articulating complex constitutional issues. Ultimately, the court upheld the doctrine of the **basic structure**, a concept that was born out of the clear, concise, and powerful legal writing that laid the groundwork for the arguments.

Components of an Effective Brief

A well-written **brief** typically contains the following components:

- **Statement of Facts**: A concise summary of the relevant facts of the case, focusing only on those that are necessary to understand the legal issues.

- **Issues Presented**: The legal questions that the court must decide.

- **Argument**: The core of the brief, where the legal reasoning, precedents, and statutes are discussed. This section uses **IRAC** (Issue, Rule, Application, Conclusion) as its framework.

- **Conclusion**: A brief summary that restates the desired outcome.

In legal writing, the brief must be structured logically, but it must also be persuasive. It is not enough to present the facts and laws, you must weave them together in a way that leads the court to the desired conclusion.

Memorandum: Internal Legal Analysis

A **memorandum** (or **memo**) is a written document used primarily for internal legal analysis. While briefs are intended for external audiences (like courts), memos are typically used within a law firm or a legal department to analyze a particular issue, offering recommendations based on the law.

Case Study: The Use of Memoranda in the Aadhaar Case

In the **Aadhaar Case (Justice K.S. Puttaswamy v. Union of India, 2018)**, memoranda played a critical role in shaping the legal strategies used by the petitioners and respondents. Legal teams prepared internal memos to assess the constitutionality of the Aadhaar scheme in relation to privacy rights. These memos analyzed previous case law, including the landmark **Privacy Judgment (2017)**, and helped attorneys structure their arguments in court.

The use of memoranda in complex cases like Aadhaar demonstrates how essential internal legal analysis is in crafting courtroom strategies. While the memo is not submitted to the court, it serves as the backbone of legal reasoning and decision-making.

Structure of a Legal Memorandum

A legal **memorandum** generally includes:

- **Heading**: Includes information such as the subject of the memo, the recipient, and the date.

- **Question Presented**: A brief statement of the legal issue that the memo addresses.

- **Brief Answer**: A concise summary of the conclusion reached in the memo.

- **Facts**: A summary of the relevant facts that form the basis of the legal question.

- **Discussion/Analysis**: The most extensive section, where the legal issue is analyzed using statutes, case law, and other legal authorities.

- **Conclusion**: A summary of the analysis and the recommended course of action.

The purpose of a memo is not persuasion, as it is with a brief, but clear and objective analysis. However, like all legal writing, clarity and precision are paramount.

Motion: Requesting Court Action

A **motion** is a formal request made to the court for a specific action or decision. Motions can be made at various stages of a case and cover a wide range of procedural and substantive issues. Whether it's a motion to dismiss, a motion for summary judgment, or a motion to compel discovery, the vocabulary of motions is critical in shaping the trajectory of a case.

Case Study: Sanjeev Kumar v. State of Haryana (2020)

In **Sanjeev Kumar v. State of Haryana**, a motion was filed to dismiss a case based on a procedural issue. The defendant's motion argued that the charges were barred by the statute of limitations. The court ultimately denied the motion, stating that certain tolling provisions applied to extend the limitations period.

This case underscores the importance of understanding the **motion** process. A motion can lead to the dismissal of a case before it even reaches trial, but it must be based on a solid legal foundation. In this instance, the defendant's motion failed because it did not take into account the legal exceptions that extended the statute of limitations.

Common Types of Motions

Some common **motions** in legal writing include:

- **Motion to Dismiss**: Filed when a party believes the case should be dismissed for legal reasons, such as lack of jurisdiction or failure to state a claim.

- **Motion for Summary Judgment**: Filed when one party believes there is no dispute of material fact, and they are entitled to judgment as a matter of law.

- **Motion to Compel**: Filed when one party is not complying with discovery requests, and the opposing party seeks a court order compelling compliance.

Each type of motion has its own legal standard, and effective legal writing in motions requires a deep understanding of both the facts of the case and the procedural rules governing the motion.

Opinion: Judicial Reasoning in Writing

A judicial **opinion** is a written explanation of the court's decision in a case. It not only resolves the dispute between the parties but also sets a precedent for future cases. The language of judicial opinions is critical because it interprets the law, applies it to the facts, and often sets new legal standards.

Case Study: Olga Tellis v. Bombay Municipal Corporation (1985)

In the landmark case of **Olga Tellis v. Bombay Municipal Corporation**, the Supreme Court of India issued an opinion that expanded the scope of **Article 21 of the Constitution** (the right to life and personal liberty) to include the right to livelihood. The court's opinion was written in clear and powerful language, stating that the right to life is not merely the right to exist, but the right to live with dignity.

The opinion not only resolved the immediate dispute about the eviction of pavement dwellers but also had far-reaching implications for how the courts interpret the **right to life** in future cases. The clarity and depth of the court's writing in this opinion helped shape Indian constitutional law.

Structure of a Judicial Opinion

A judicial **opinion** typically includes:

- A summary of the facts and the legal issues before the court.

- **Legal Discussion**: An analysis of the relevant laws, including statutes and precedents, applied to the facts of the case.

- **Holding**: The court's decision regarding the legal issues.

- **Reasoning**: The explanation of why the court reached its decision, often including interpretations of statutes and precedents.

- **Conclusion**: A brief statement that reiterates the court's final ruling.

Judicial opinions are the cornerstone of legal precedent. The way they are written can influence legal interpretations for generations, making them one of the most significant forms of legal writing.

Pleading: The Foundation of Litigation

Pleadings are the formal written statements filed by the parties in a lawsuit that state their claims and defenses. The most common types of pleadings are the **complaint** (filed by the plaintiff) and the **answer** (filed by the defendant). Pleadings set the stage for the litigation, laying out the legal and factual issues that the court must resolve.

Case Study: Vishakha v. State of Rajasthan (1997)

In **Vishakha v. State of Rajasthan**, the pleadings were instrumental in framing the legal issues surrounding sexual

harassment in the workplace. The petitioners, a group of women's rights organizations, filed a **writ petition** under **Article 32 of the Indian Constitution**, seeking to enforce fundamental rights. The pleadings outlined the lack of a legal framework to address sexual harassment and called on the court to issue guidelines to protect women in the workplace.

The court's decision, known as the **Vishakha Guidelines,** established new standards for preventing sexual harassment in the workplace. This case illustrates the power of well-drafted pleadings to shape legal discourse and bring about systemic change.

Elements of a Complaint

A well-structured **complaint** includes the following elements:

- **Caption**: Identifies the court, parties, and case number.

- **Jurisdiction**: Explains why the court has the authority to hear the case.

- **Statement of Facts**: A clear and concise account of the events that give rise to the legal claim.

- **Causes of Action**: The specific legal claims being made (e.g., breach of contract, negligence).

- **Prayer for Relief**: A statement of what the plaintiff is asking the court to do (e.g., award damages, issue an injunction).

The **answer**, filed by the defendant, responds to each of the allegations made in the complaint, either admitting, denying, or claiming insufficient knowledge to admit or deny the allegation.

Pleadings are essential in defining the scope of the dispute and ensuring that both parties have a clear understanding of the issues at hand. The precision and clarity with which pleadings are drafted can significantly influence the direction of a case.

The Language of Legal Writing: Precision, Clarity, and Power

Legal writing demands not only a command of vocabulary but also a deep understanding of how to use words with **precision**, **clarity**, and **power**. Unlike other forms of writing, where creativity and expression may take precedence, legal writing must adhere to strict rules of language and structure.

The Importance of Plain Language

While legal writing has historically been criticized for its complexity, modern trends emphasize the use of **plain language**. Judges and lawyers alike are moving toward writing that is simple, clear, and accessible. This shift recognizes that the purpose of legal writing is not to impress with jargon, but to communicate ideas effectively.

In **State of Tamil Nadu v. K. Balu (2017)**, the Supreme Court of India delivered a judgment that was notable for its **clarity**. The court struck down the sale of alcohol along national highways, using simple, straightforward language to explain the dangers of drunk driving. The judgment was widely praised for its accessibility and its direct connection to public safety concerns.

Using Legal Terms Appropriately

While clarity is important, legal writing must still use the correct **legal terms** to convey specific meanings. Words like **res judicata**, **estoppel**, and **stare decisis** have precise legal definitions that cannot be substituted with simpler words without losing their meaning.

For example, the concept of **res judicata**, which prevents the same dispute from being litigated multiple times, was crucial in the case of **Satyadhan Ghosal v. Deorajin Debi (1960)**. The Supreme Court applied the principle to dismiss a second lawsuit that raised the same issues as a previously decided case.

In this sense, legal writing is about finding a balance between clarity and technical accuracy. While legal terms must be used where necessary, they should be explained clearly to avoid confusion.

The Art of Legal Writing

Mastering the vocabulary of legal writing is not just about knowing terms, it is about understanding how those terms fit into a broader framework of justice, fairness, and clarity. Whether drafting a brief, preparing a motion, or writing a judicial opinion, every word matters. Precision is the foundation of legal writing, but so too is the ability to communicate effectively and persuasively.

The case studies we have explored in this chapter demonstrate the power of legal writing to shape decisions, influence courts, and bring about legal reform. By mastering the vocabulary and structure of legal documents, you will be better equipped to advocate for your clients, shape legal arguments, and contribute to the ongoing evolution of the law.

"The law is not only a set of rules but a conversation, a conversation where every word must be chosen with care, for it carries the weight of justice."

\- **Justice P.N. Bhagwati**

Exercises and Practical Applications

1. Draft a Brief:

Draft a brief for a hypothetical case involving a breach of contract. Focus on presenting the facts, legal issues, and argument in a clear and persuasive manner.

2. Analyze a Judicial Opinion:

Select a judicial opinion from a recent case and analyze the structure of the opinion. Identify the holding, reasoning, and the language used to convey the court's decision.

3. Write a Legal Memorandum:

Prepare a legal memorandum analyzing a hypothetical issue involving intellectual property rights. Use case law and statutes to support your analysis.

These exercises will help you develop a deep understanding of legal writing vocabulary and its application, preparing you for real-world legal writing tasks.

Chapter 18: The Language of Legal Communication

"Legal communication is not just about conveying information; it is about building trust, establishing credibility, and persuading the audience."

\- **Cicero**

The Heart of Legal Practice

Legal communication is more than a set of skills, it is the lifeblood of law itself. In every courtroom, in every negotiation, and in every written document, the ability to convey ideas clearly and persuasively determines outcomes. Legal communication is about more than just words; it is about connecting arguments to people, ideas to justice, and decisions to consequences.

Whether we are speaking in a courtroom, writing a legal opinion, or negotiating a contract, every word must be chosen with care. This chapter will delve deep into the **language of legal communication**, exploring terms like **argument**, **objection**, **cross-examination**, **closing statement**, and **evidence presentation**. Through real-world case studies and examples, we will unpack how legal professionals use language to advocate, persuade, and achieve justice.

In the pages ahead, we will explore not just the mechanics of legal communication but the philosophy behind it. We will examine how words are used to challenge power, protect the vulnerable, and shape the decisions that influence society. Ultimately, this chapter aims to equip you with the tools to communicate effectively in any legal setting, with precision, clarity, and impact.

Argument: The Core of Advocacy

At the heart of every legal case lies the **argument**, the structured presentation of reasons, laws, and evidence that supports one side of a dispute. Legal arguments are crafted through a careful combination of logic, legal precedent, and persuasive language.

Case Study: Kesavananda Bharati v. State of Kerala (1973)

In one of the most significant constitutional law cases in Indian history, **Kesavananda Bharati v. State of Kerala**, the argument presented by both sides had a lasting impact on the interpretation of the Constitution. The petitioners argued that the Parliament could not alter the "basic structure" of the Constitution, while the government contended that its powers to amend the Constitution were absolute. The arguments were not only rooted in constitutional text but also appealed to broader principles of democracy and governance.

The Supreme Court ultimately accepted the **basic structure doctrine**, a decision that has shaped Indian constitutional law for decades. The power of argument in this case was not just in the words used, but in how they resonated with the values of the Constitution itself.

Components of a Persuasive Argument

A well-constructed **legal argument** includes:

- Clearly states the legal issue at hand.

- **Statement of Facts**: Presents the relevant facts in a way that supports the argument.

- **Legal Reasoning**: Applies the law to the facts, using legal precedents and statutes to build a case.

- **Counterarguments**: Anticipates and addresses the opposing party's arguments.

- **Conclusion**: Summarizes the argument and reiterates the desired outcome.

In legal communication, **persuasion** is key. A well-presented argument must not only follow the rules of logic but also appeal to the emotions and values of the audience, whether a judge, jury, or opposing counsel.

Objection: Challenging Evidence and Testimony

In the heat of a courtroom trial, the term **objection** becomes a powerful tool. Objections are used to challenge the admissibility of evidence or the propriety of a question posed during examination. They are based on specific legal grounds and can be pivotal in shaping the outcome of a case.

Case Study: Nirbhaya Rape Case (2012)

During the trial of the **Nirbhaya Rape Case**, the defense raised several objections regarding the admissibility of certain forensic evidence and witness testimony. The prosecution, in turn, argued for the relevance and importance of that evidence. The court had to navigate these objections carefully, balancing the rights of the accused with the necessity of presenting a complete picture of the crime.

This case highlighted the strategic use of objections in a high-stakes trial. While objections are often procedural, they can have profound substantive effects, influencing what the judge or jury hears and ultimately, what conclusions they draw.

Common Grounds for Objections

In legal practice, objections can be raised on various grounds, including:

- **Relevance**: The evidence or testimony must directly relate to the issues in the case.

- **Hearsay**: Statements made outside of court that are offered to prove the truth of the matter asserted are generally inadmissible unless an exception applies.

- **Speculation**: Witnesses are prohibited from speculating or guessing about facts that are not within their direct knowledge.

- **Leading Questions**: On direct examination, leading questions, those that suggest their own answer, are generally not permitted.

Knowing when and how to object is critical in courtroom communication. It requires a deep understanding of both substantive and procedural law, as well as the ability to act swiftly and assertively.

Cross-Examination: The Art of Uncovering Truth

Cross-examination is one of the most powerful tools available to a lawyer. It allows the questioning of the opposing party's witnesses to test the accuracy, reliability, and credibility of their testimony. Cross-examination is not just about challenging facts but about revealing inconsistencies, biases, or errors that could undermine the opposing side's case.

Case Study: Jessica Lal Murder Case (1999)

In the **Jessica Lal Murder Case**, the defense attempted to discredit the testimony of key witnesses during cross-examination. The prosecution's witnesses had testified that the accused had shot Jessica Lal in public view. The defense sought to highlight inconsistencies in the witnesses' recollections, casting doubt on the reliability of their statements.

Ultimately, however, the cross-examination failed to dismantle the prosecution's case, and the accused was convicted. This case underscores the importance of cross-examination in testing the strength of witness testimony, while also demonstrating that a well-prepared prosecution can withstand aggressive questioning.

Effective Techniques in Cross-Examination

In cross-examination, the goal is not to argue with the witness but to control the narrative by asking precise, closed-ended questions. Techniques include:

- **Leading Questions**: The examiner asks questions that suggest the answer, steering the witness toward admissions that weaken their testimony.

- **Impeachment**: Highlighting inconsistencies between the witness's current testimony and prior statements.

- **Focusing on Specific Facts**: Narrowing the scope of questioning to specific, critical facts that can be more easily challenged.

Cross-examination is an art that requires sharp attention to detail and a deep understanding of the case. A well-executed cross-examination can dismantle the opposition's case, while a poorly executed one can reinforce the opposing side's narrative.

Closing Statement: Persuading the Judge or Jury

The **closing statement** is the lawyer's final opportunity to address the court, summarizing the evidence and reinforcing the key arguments. This is a crucial moment in any trial, as it allows the lawyer to frame the narrative one last time before the judge or jury deliberates.

Case Study: O.J. Simpson Trial (1995)

The **closing statements** in the **O.J. Simpson trial** are often cited as textbook examples of how to use language, emotion, and logic to persuade a jury. Both the defense and the prosecution made impassioned final arguments, with the defense famously urging the jury, "If it doesn't fit, you must acquit," in reference to the glove evidence. This phrase became emblematic of the defense's strategy to create reasonable doubt in the minds of the jurors.

The closing statement in this trial showcased the power of succinct, memorable language in persuading a jury. The defense's closing statement, while brief, was rhetorically effective, and it played a significant role in Simpson's acquittal.

Crafting a Compelling Closing Statement

An effective **closing statement** should:

- **Summarize the Evidence**: Recap the most important pieces of evidence and explain how they support your case.

- **Address Weaknesses**: Acknowledge any weaknesses in your case and explain why they do not undermine your overall argument.

- **Appeal to Emotions and Logic**: A closing statement should not only present logical reasoning but also appeal to the values and emotions of the judge or jury.

- **Call to Action**: End with a clear and compelling request for the desired outcome, whether it be a conviction, acquittal, or a favorable ruling.

In the legal world, words matter most in the moments that define the final outcome. The closing statement is a powerful reminder of the importance of communication in achieving justice.

Evidence Presentation: Building the Foundation for Argument

The **presentation of evidence** is fundamental to legal communication, as it forms the basis upon which arguments are built. Whether in the form of witness testimony, documents, or physical evidence, how evidence is introduced and explained can make or break a case.

Case Study: Aarushi Talwar Murder Case (2008)

The **Aarushi Talwar Murder Case** involved significant controversy over the handling and presentation of forensic evidence. Questions were raised about the collection and interpretation of DNA evidence, as well as the reliability of certain witness testimonies. The way in which the evidence was presented by both the prosecution and defense became a critical factor in the outcome of the trial.

In this case, the **communication of forensic evidence** was particularly significant. The manner in which evidence is presented, its clarity, context, and coherence, determines its impact on the judge or jury.

Rules of Evidence

The **rules of evidence** govern how evidence can be presented in court. Some key rules include:

- **Relevance**: Evidence must directly relate to the issues being decided in the case.

- **Admissibility**: Certain types of evidence, such as hearsay or privileged communication, may not be admissible.

- **Chain of Custody**: For physical evidence, it is important to establish a chain of custody to prove that the evidence has not been tampered with.

Effective evidence presentation requires both legal knowledge and clear communication. Lawyers must ensure that their evidence is not only admissible but also understandable and persuasive.

The Importance of Tone and Professionalism

Legal communication is not just about what is said, it is about **how** it is said. The **tone** of legal communication must always be professional, respectful, and focused on the issues at hand. Whether in court, in written documents, or in negotiations, the tone of legal communication can significantly impact its effectiveness.

Case Study: S. Rangarajan v. P. Jagjivan Ram (1989)

In the case of **S. Rangarajan v. P. Jagjivan Ram**, the tone of legal arguments before the Supreme Court of India played a significant role. The case dealt with the freedom of speech and expression, particularly in the context of film censorship. The arguments were forceful yet respectful, and the court ultimately ruled in favor of freedom of expression, emphasizing the importance of open debate in a democratic society.

The tone adopted by lawyers in this case reflected the gravity of the issues involved and the need for careful, respectful communication in matters concerning fundamental rights.

Professionalism in Legal Communication

Professionalism in legal communication involves:

- **Respectful Language**: Avoiding personal attacks or inflammatory language.

- **Objectivity**: Keeping the focus on legal arguments and evidence rather than emotional appeals or rhetoric.

- **Clarity and Precision**: Using language that is clear, precise, and free from ambiguity.

- **Ethical Conduct**: Upholding the ethical standards of the legal profession, including honesty and integrity in all communications.

A lawyer's tone and demeanor are as important as the content of their communication. Respectful, clear, and professional language ensures that the legal process remains fair and just.

Mastering Legal Communication

Legal communication is a powerful tool. It has the ability to change lives, alter the course of justice, and shape society. Whether in a courtroom, a boardroom, or a written document, the language of the law must always be clear, precise, and respectful.

The case studies and concepts discussed in this chapter illustrate the complexity and nuance of legal communication. From the construction of persuasive arguments to the art of cross-examination, from the power of objections to the finality of closing statements, every word spoken or written in the legal field carries weight.

As future lawyers, mastering the language of legal communication will enable you to advocate effectively, defend justly, and, most importantly, contribute to the greater goal of justice in society.

"The law is not just a set of rules but a conversation, a dialogue between rights and responsibilities, justice and power. And in this dialogue, the words we choose can change the world."

\- **Justice V.R. Krishna Iyer**

Exercises and Practical Applications

1. Mock Cross-Examination:

Participate in a mock cross-examination where you challenge the credibility of a witness. Focus on using precise language and asking leading questions to reveal inconsistencies in testimony.

2. **Draft a Closing Statement**:

Write a closing statement for a hypothetical criminal trial. Summarize the evidence and make a compelling argument for the outcome you are seeking.

3. Analyze an Objection:

Select a transcript from a real court case and analyze the objections raised during the trial. Were they valid? How did the objections shape the outcome of the case?

These exercises will help you apply the principles of legal communication in practical settings, preparing you for the real-world challenges of advocacy, negotiation, and courtroom communication.

Chapter 19: Latin Phrases Every Lawyer Should Know

"Latin is the language of law, and while its use may be declining, its wisdom endures. Understanding Latin maxims is essential for grasping the foundations of legal thought."

- **John Selden**

Why Latin Still Echoes in Modern Law

Latin is often referred to as the language of law. For centuries, it has shaped legal discourse and continues to be the foundation for many legal principles and doctrines. As young lawyers stepping into a world governed by rules, precedent, and language, an understanding of key Latin phrases is not just beneficial, it is essential.

Why is Latin still relevant in modern law? Because these phrases encapsulate complex legal ideas with remarkable precision. Terms like **stare decisis**, **res ipsa loquitur**, and **actus reus** are not just remnants of an ancient tongue; they are the pillars that support legal reasoning. In many ways, Latin serves as a universal language in law, connecting practitioners across jurisdictions and legal traditions.

This chapter will dive deep into essential Latin phrases, explaining their meaning, providing real-world case studies, and showing how they are applied in practice. By the end of this chapter, these phrases will not just be terms you memorize for exams, they will become part of the way you think and practice law.

Stare Decisis: Let the Decision Stand

One of the most fundamental principles of common law, **stare decisis** means "to stand by things decided." This doctrine dictates that courts should follow precedents, previous rulings, in similar cases to ensure consistency and stability in the law.

Case Study: Kesavananda Bharati v. State of Kerala (1973)

In **Kesavananda Bharati v. State of Kerala**, the Supreme Court of India faced a constitutional crisis. Could Parliament amend every part of the Constitution, including its fundamental features? The court's decision created the **basic structure doctrine**, which limits Parliament's power to alter the Constitution's core principles.

But why is this relevant to **stare decisis**? Because in future cases, the basic structure doctrine became a binding precedent. For example, in **Minerva Mills v. Union of India (1980)**, the court reaffirmed the Kesavananda judgment, applying the principle of **stare decisis** to protect the basic structure of the Constitution.

This principle ensures that the law remains consistent over time. It balances the need for stability with the need for legal evolution, ensuring that past wisdom informs future decisions.

Importance of Stare Decisis in Legal Practice

When arguing a case, lawyers often rely on the principle of **stare decisis** to support their positions. Precedents, once established, are powerful tools, as courts generally hesitate to overturn previous rulings unless there is a compelling reason. Understanding how to use past rulings effectively can be the difference between winning and losing a case.

Res Ipsa Loquitur: The Thing Speaks for Itself

In tort law, the doctrine of **res ipsa loquitur** allows plaintiffs to infer negligence from the very nature of an accident, even when direct evidence is unavailable. It translates to "the thing speaks for itself," and is often invoked when the cause of injury is obvious, though the specific act of negligence is not.

Case Study: Shyam Sundar v. State of Rajasthan (1974)

In **Shyam Sundar v. State of Rajasthan**, the plaintiffs were injured due to the collapse of a wall during a festival. There was no direct evidence of negligence on the part of the event organizers. However, the court applied the doctrine of **res ipsa loquitur**, reasoning that such an accident would not have occurred if proper safety measures had been in place.

The court's application of **res ipsa loquitur** allowed the plaintiffs to shift the burden of proof to the defendant, demonstrating the doctrine's practical importance. When an accident's circumstances strongly suggest negligence, this Latin phrase empowers the injured party by making it easier to establish fault.

The Three Requirements for Res Ipsa Loquitur

For **res ipsa loquitur** to apply, three conditions must generally be met:

- **The event must be of a kind that ordinarily does not occur in the absence of negligence.**

- **The event must have been caused by something within the defendant's control.**

- **The plaintiff must not have contributed to the event.**

This doctrine simplifies the litigation process in negligence cases by focusing on the event's circumstances rather than requiring specific evidence of a negligent act. Lawyers invoking this principle effectively argue that the event itself demonstrates negligence.

Actus Reus and Mens Rea: The Guilty Act and the Guilty Mind

In criminal law, both **actus reus** (the guilty act) and **mens rea** (the guilty mind) must be proven to establish liability. These two terms form the foundation of criminal liability, and without both elements, a defendant cannot typically be found guilty of a crime.

Case Study: R v. Cunningham (1957)

In the English case of **R v. Cunningham**, the defendant tore a gas meter off a wall to steal money, causing a gas leak that endangered lives. The court had to determine whether the defendant acted with **mens rea**, the requisite mental state. They ruled that **recklessness** in this case was sufficient to establish **mens rea**. Cunningham's **actus reus** (the physical act of removing the gas meter) combined with his reckless disregard for the consequences satisfied the elements of a crime.

This case underscores the need for both **actus reus** and **mens rea** in criminal law. Without proof of a guilty mind, an otherwise harmful act might not be punishable.

Actus Reus and Mens Rea in Indian Law

In India, these principles are embedded in the **Indian Penal Code (IPC)**. For example, **Section 299** of the IPC defines culpable homicide as causing death with the intent to kill or cause bodily harm (mens rea), coupled with an actual act that leads to death (actus reus). Understanding the interplay between these two elements is crucial for any criminal lawyer.

Ultra Vires: Beyond Powers

Ultra vires means "beyond the powers," and it is a doctrine used to challenge actions taken by a government body, corporation, or individual that exceed the legal authority granted to them.

Case Study: State of Rajasthan v. Union of India (1977)

In **State of Rajasthan v. Union of India**, the Supreme Court of India had to determine whether the central government had acted **ultra vires** its constitutional powers when it imposed President's Rule in several states. The court ruled that while the central government had broad powers under **Article 356** of the Indian Constitution, these powers were not absolute and could not be used arbitrarily.

The concept of **ultra vires** is critical in ensuring that all actions by authorities remain within their legally defined limits. This doctrine provides a check against the abuse of power, protecting both citizens and the legal system from overreach.

Applications in Corporate Law

Ultra vires also plays a role in corporate law. If a corporation acts outside the scope of its corporate charter, those actions may be deemed **ultra vires** and void. For instance, if a company established for manufacturing decides to engage in banking without proper authorization, its actions can be challenged as **ultra vires**.

This phrase is a safeguard, ensuring that entities do not overstep the boundaries of their legal authority.

Habeas Corpus: You Shall Have the Body

Habeas corpus is one of the most important legal principles in protecting individual liberty. It allows a person to challenge unlawful detention or imprisonment. The phrase means "you shall have the body," and it commands the detaining authority to produce the person before a court to justify the detention.

Case Study: ADM Jabalpur v. Shivkant Shukla (1976)

The infamous **ADM Jabalpur v. Shivkant Shukla** case, also known as the **Habeas Corpus Case**, arose during India's Emergency (1975-1977), when the government suspended many fundamental rights, including the right to challenge detention. The petitioners filed **habeas corpus** petitions challenging their unlawful arrests.

In a controversial ruling, the Supreme Court held that during the Emergency, even the right to file **habeas corpus** petitions could be suspended. This decision was widely criticized, and in the years that followed, it became a symbol of judicial capitulation to executive power. The ruling has since been overruled in principle, reaffirming **habeas corpus** as a fundamental safeguard against arbitrary detention.

Habeas Corpus in Modern Practice

Today, **habeas corpus** remains a powerful tool for protecting personal liberty. In India, Article 32 and Article 226 of the Constitution provide for **habeas corpus** petitions in the Supreme Court and High Courts, respectively. This writ is essential in ensuring that no person is deprived of their liberty without legal justification.

Ex Post Facto: After the Fact

The principle of **ex post facto** laws prohibits the application of laws retroactively. In other words, a person cannot be punished for an act that was not a crime when it was committed.

Case Study: Keshavan Madhava Menon v. State of Bombay (1951)

In **Keshavan Madhava Menon v. State of Bombay**, the petitioner was charged under a law that was enacted

after the alleged offense occurred. The Supreme Court of India ruled that **ex post facto** laws could not be applied to criminal cases, as doing so would violate the principle of fairness in legal proceedings. The court relied on Article 20(1) of the Indian Constitution, which explicitly prohibits the retrospective application of criminal laws.

The Importance of Ex Post Facto Protections

The prohibition against **ex post facto** laws protects individuals from being unfairly punished by laws enacted after the fact. This principle ensures that people are only held accountable for violations of laws that were in force at the time of their actions, preventing arbitrary punishment and ensuring fairness in criminal justice.

Ratio Decidendi and Obiter Dicta: The Reasoning and the Commentary

When courts issue judgments, they often include both the **ratio decidendi** and **obiter dicta**. **Ratio decidendi** refers to the legal reasoning that forms the basis of the court's decision and is binding in future cases, while **obiter dicta** are remarks or observations made by the judge that are not essential to the decision and are not legally binding.

Case Study: Golaknath v. State of Punjab (1967)

In **Golaknath v. State of Punjab**, the Supreme Court of India addressed whether Parliament had the power to amend fundamental rights under the Constitution. The **ratio decidendi** was that

Parliament could not amend fundamental rights, a principle later overturned in the **Kesavananda Bharati case**.

However, the **obiter dicta** in the Golaknath judgment also provided significant insights into the court's views on constitutional amendments, even though they were not binding in future cases. Lawyers often examine both the **ratio decidendi** and **obiter dicta** when analyzing judgments, as the latter can influence future legal arguments and interpretations.

Using Ratio and Obiter in Legal Arguments

Understanding the distinction between **ratio decidendi** and **obiter dicta** is crucial for any lawyer. When citing cases, it is important to focus on the **ratio** as it is the legally binding part of the judgment. However, **obiter dicta** can be persuasive, especially if made by a respected judge or in a significant case.

De Facto and De Jure: In Fact and In Law

De facto means "in fact," while **de jure** means "in law." These terms are often used to distinguish between situations that exist in reality and those that are recognized by law.

Case Study: Ganga Ram Moolchandani v. State of Rajasthan (2001)

In **Ganga Ram Moolchandani v. State of Rajasthan**, the court dealt with a dispute over the appointment of a public official. The individual had been acting in the position **de facto** (in practice) but did not hold the title **de jure** (in law). The court ruled that while the **de facto** actions taken by the individual were valid, his lack of **de jure** authority raised questions about the legality of certain decisions.

This case highlights the importance of distinguishing between **de facto** and **de jure** authority, especially in administrative and governance matters.

Latin as the Eternal Language of Law

The Latin phrases explored in this chapter are more than relics of a bygone era, they are living, breathing concepts that continue to shape the practice of law. Understanding these phrases is essential for any lawyer, not just for academic purposes but because they encapsulate fundamental legal principles that are applied every day in courts around the world.

From the stability of **stare decisis** to the protection of liberty in **habeas corpus**, Latin phrases provide a framework that makes the law consistent, predictable, and fair. As you continue your legal journey, these phrases will become part of the foundation upon which you build your arguments, craft your defenses, and seek justice.

> *"The wisdom of the past speaks to us through the language of Latin. It reminds us that law is not merely a set of rules, but a system of justice, fairness, and morality that must stand the test of time."*
>
> \- **Justice Oliver Wendell Holmes**

Exercises and Practical Applications

1. Analyze a Judgment:

Select a recent Supreme Court judgment and identify the **ratio decidendi** and **obiter dicta**. Discuss how both the reasoning and the commentary might influence future cases.

2. Draft a Legal Opinion:

Using the principles of **res ipsa loquitur**, write a legal opinion on a hypothetical tort case where negligence is inferred from the facts.

3. Examine a Case for Stare Decisis:

Find a case where **stare decisis** played a significant role in the decision. Analyze how the court relied on past precedents and whether any new legal principles were introduced.

By completing these exercises, you will deepen your understanding of Latin legal phrases and their practical applications, preparing you for real-world legal challenges where precision in language and reasoning is crucial.

Chapter 20: Legal Maxims and Their Application

"Maxims are the condensed good sense of nations."

- **Lord John Russell**

The Wisdom of Legal Maxims

The law is an ancient craft, honed and shaped over centuries. While statutes, judgments, and regulations govern our legal systems today, beneath these modern constructs lie enduring principles that continue to influence decisions in courts worldwide. Legal maxims, short, pithy statements that encapsulate fundamental legal principles, are among these foundational tools. They distill the complexities of law into simple, timeless truths, offering guidance to judges, lawyers, and scholars alike.

Legal maxims are more than just linguistic relics from Roman law or medieval legal philosophy; they are the foundation stones that continue to support contemporary legal reasoning. In their brevity, they capture profound wisdom. Maxims like **ignorantia juris non excusat** (ignorance of the law is no excuse) or **nemo dat quod non habet** (one cannot give what one does not have) are as relevant today as they were when first conceived.

This chapter will explore key legal maxims, their meaning, and their application in real-world cases. By understanding these maxims and the underlying principles they reflect, you will be equipped to navigate the complexities of law with a deeper appreciation for its philosophical roots. In the words of Mahatma

Gandhi, ***"Law means to work for justice,"*** and maxims often provide the roadmap to that justice.

Ignorantia Juris Non Excusat: Ignorance of the Law Is No Excuse

One of the most fundamental maxims in law, **ignorantia juris non excusat**, stands for the idea that a person cannot escape liability simply because they were unaware of the law. This principle ensures that individuals are held accountable for their actions, even if they claim to have been ignorant of the legal implications.

Case Study: K. Veeraswami v. Union of India (1991)

In the landmark case of **K. Veeraswami v. Union of India**, the issue of ignorance of the law was brought to the forefront. Veeraswami, a high-ranking public servant, was charged with amassing wealth beyond his known sources of income, violating anti-corruption laws. His defense argued that he was unaware of certain statutory obligations regarding the declaration of assets.

The Supreme Court of India rejected this argument, reaffirming the principle that **ignorantia juris non excusat**. The court held that ignorance of the law cannot be an excuse, especially for someone in a position of power and responsibility. The case underscored the importance of accountability and the expectation that citizens, particularly public officials, must know the laws that govern them.

Application in Everyday Life

This maxim ensures that the law applies equally to everyone. Whether you are a layperson unaware of a tax filing requirement or a corporate executive neglecting compliance regulations, ignorance does not exempt you from legal consequences. It is a reminder that laws are made to be followed and that individuals have a duty to acquaint themselves with the legal framework within which they live and work.

However, there are limits. Courts are often sympathetic in cases where laws are exceptionally obscure or ambiguous, although they rarely allow ignorance as a full defense. This maxim reflects the importance of fairness in the legal system while maintaining the integrity of its enforcement.

Nemo Dat Quod Non Habet: One Cannot Give What One Does Not Have

The principle of **nemo dat quod non habet** protects property rights by ensuring that no one can transfer more rights than they possess. This maxim is fundamental in property law, safeguarding buyers and sellers alike by ensuring that ownership and authority must be genuine and traceable.

Case Study: National Textile Corporation v. Nareshkumar Badrikumar Jagad (2011)

In **National Textile Corporation v. Nareshkumar Badrikumar Jagad**, the court applied the **nemo dat** principle in a dispute over the sale of property. The corporation had leased a piece of land from the government, but the question arose about the tenant's right to sublease. The sublessee claimed full ownership rights based on the transaction.

The Supreme Court ruled that since the National Textile Corporation did not have full ownership of the property (it was only a tenant), it could not transfer ownership rights to a third party. The court cited **nemo dat quod non habet**, emphasizing that no one can transfer rights they do not possess.

Importance in Property Transactions

In property law, **nemo dat** plays a crucial role in maintaining the integrity of ownership chains. It ensures that buyers conduct due diligence before purchasing property, particularly in real estate, where ownership history can be complex. This maxim reminds us that legal transactions must be rooted in genuine ownership; otherwise, they are void or, at best, highly questionable.

This principle is equally relevant in the sale of goods and personal property, where a seller must possess legal title to transfer ownership. It also applies in cases of theft or fraud, where the recovery of property hinges on tracing the true owner.

Audi Alteram Partem: Hear the Other Side

Audi alteram partem is one of the cornerstones of natural justice. It means that no one should be condemned, judged, or ruled against without a fair opportunity to present their case. This principle of fairness is foundational in both civil and criminal proceedings, ensuring that all parties are heard before a decision is made.

Case Study: Maneka Gandhi v. Union of India (1978)

In the landmark case of **Maneka Gandhi v. Union of India**, the petitioner's passport was impounded by the government without giving her an opportunity to be heard. Gandhi challenged this action, arguing that it violated her right to natural justice.

The Supreme Court of India agreed, ruling that the principle of **audi alteram partem** was essential to a fair legal process. The court held that the right to a hearing is a fundamental aspect of **Article 21** of the Constitution, which guarantees the right to life and personal liberty. By not allowing Gandhi to present her case before impounding her passport, the government had violated her constitutional rights.

Application in Administrative Law

The principle of **audi alteram partem** is most commonly invoked in administrative and procedural law. It ensures that government agencies, employers, and other decision-making bodies provide individuals with a chance to be heard before making decisions that affect their rights or obligations. In disciplinary actions, terminations, or even contract disputes, this maxim guarantees fairness and transparency.

In a broader sense, this maxim reflects the moral foundation of law, that justice is not just about outcomes but also about the process. Ensuring that every party has a voice is fundamental to the integrity of any legal system.

Actio Personalis Moritur Cum Persona: A Personal Action Dies with the Person

The maxim **actio personalis moritur cum persona** dictates that certain personal rights or causes of action expire upon the death of the person. This principle traditionally applied to tort claims like defamation, where the right to seek damages was considered personal and did not survive death.

Case Study: Girijanandini v. Bijendra Narain (1967)

In **Girijanandini v. Bijendra Narain**, the Supreme Court of India had to decide whether a tortious claim could continue after the death of one of the parties. The plaintiff, who had brought a claim for damages, died during the proceedings. The defendant argued that the case should be dismissed under the principle of **actio personalis moritur cum persona**.

The court held that while certain tort claims do expire upon death, claims related to property, financial recovery, or contract breaches may survive. The ruling provided a nuanced interpretation of the maxim, stating that while personal claims (like defamation or assault) may die with the person, claims related to financial or property rights often do not.

Modern-Day Application

While **actio personalis** has been limited over time, especially with the introduction of statutes that allow the estate of a deceased person to pursue certain legal claims, the principle still holds relevance. Claims for personal injuries or defamation often die with the claimant, while other claims, especially those relating to property or contract rights, may survive.

In many jurisdictions, legislative changes have reformed this maxim, allowing for actions to continue posthumously under certain conditions. However, its core philosophy remains important: personal wrongs tied to the individual's experience do not typically transcend death.

Falsus in Uno, Falsus in Omnibus: False in One Thing, False in Everything

The maxim **falsus in uno, falsus in omnibus** holds that if a witness is found to be lying about one fact, their entire testimony can be disregarded. While this principle may not be applied rigidly in modern courts, it remains a tool for evaluating the credibility of witnesses.

Case Study: State of Uttar Pradesh v. Ashok Kumar Srivastava (1992)

In **State of Uttar Pradesh v. Ashok Kumar Srivastava**, the Supreme Court dealt with the testimony of a witness who had been caught lying about specific details of the case. The defense argued that the entire testimony should be discarded under the principle of **falsus in uno**.

However, the court ruled that this maxim should not be applied strictly. The court recognized that human memory and perception are fallible, and just because a witness makes a mistake or lies about one aspect of their testimony, it does not necessarily mean that their entire testimony is unreliable. This marked a departure from the strict application of the maxim, focusing instead on a more balanced assessment of evidence.

Credibility in Modern Trials

Modern courts are more flexible in applying **falsus in uno, falsus in omnibus**, preferring to weigh the credibility of witnesses more holistically. However, the principle still provides a cautionary note: honesty is paramount in legal proceedings, and witnesses who are found to be deceitful risk undermining their entire testimony.

This maxim is less about strict application and more about encouraging truthfulness in the courtroom. Its relevance today lies in its role as a reminder that credibility is the cornerstone of justice.

Volenti Non Fit Injuria:
To One Who Volunteers, No Harm Is Done

Volenti non fit injuria is a defense in tort law that holds that a person who willingly accepts the risk of harm cannot later sue for damages. This principle often arises in cases involving dangerous activities where participants are aware of the risks involved.

Case Study: Wooldridge v. Sumner (1963)

In the English case of **Wooldridge v. Sumner**, a photographer was injured while covering a horse race. The plaintiff argued that the rider was negligent, but the defense invoked **volenti non fit**

injuria, arguing that the photographer had voluntarily assumed the risk by standing close to the racecourse.

The court ruled in favor of the defendant, holding that **volenti non fit injuria** applied because the photographer had willingly exposed himself to the risks inherent in his profession. This case highlighted the importance of consent and risk in tort law, providing a clear example of how the maxim operates.

Application in Sports and High-Risk Activities

This maxim is frequently applied in sports law, where participants voluntarily assume certain risks inherent in the activity. For example, a football player cannot sue for injuries sustained in a normal tackle, as the risk is considered part of the game. However, **volenti non fit injuria** does not apply when harm results from reckless or intentional conduct beyond the scope of the activity.

The maxim serves as a balancing tool in tort law, ensuring that individuals are not unjustly compensated for harm they willingly risked, while still holding others accountable for negligent or reckless actions.

Equity Aids the Vigilant, Not Those Who Sleep on Their Rights

This principle emphasizes that the law favors individuals who actively protect their rights and does not assist those who neglect them. In essence, it means that one cannot claim a legal remedy if they have unreasonably delayed in asserting their rights, leading to a doctrine known as **laches**.

Case Study: M.R. Prabhakar and Others v. Canara Bank (2012)

In **M.R. Prabhakar and Others v. Canara Bank**, the plaintiffs delayed filing their claim for several years, arguing that they had been wronged by the bank's actions. The bank invoked the doctrine of **laches**, asserting that the plaintiffs had "slept on their rights" and thus should be barred from seeking relief.

The Supreme Court of India agreed with the bank, ruling that the plaintiffs' long delay in asserting their rights demonstrated a lack of vigilance. The court applied the maxim **equity aids the vigilant**, highlighting that equity requires timely action and that justice cannot serve those who neglect their legal duties.

Modern Implications of Laches

In both civil and equity law, **laches** prevents claimants from waiting too long to seek a remedy. This doctrine ensures fairness to the defendant, who may be prejudiced by the plaintiff's delay. By requiring timely action, the maxim upholds the integrity of legal proceedings, ensuring that justice is neither rushed nor unnecessarily delayed.

The Timeless Wisdom of Legal Maxims

Legal maxims are more than just Latin phrases or academic curiosities; they are the distilled essence of legal wisdom, refined through centuries of judicial thought. These maxims serve as guideposts, helping legal practitioners navigate the complexities of the law with clarity and consistency. Whether it's protecting property rights through **nemo dat quod non habet** or ensuring fairness in legal proceedings with **audi alteram partem**, these principles continue to shape the decisions made in courtrooms around the world.

As you move forward in your legal journey, remember that these maxims are not just abstract concepts but practical tools that can be applied in real-world situations. Their wisdom lies in their simplicity, and their strength lies in their universality.

"The law is not just a set of rules but a reflection of our shared human values. And in these timeless maxims, we find the heart of justice."

\- **Justice P.N. Bhagwati**

Exercises and Practical Applications

1. Research a Legal Maxim:

Choose a legal maxim not covered in this chapter and research its origin, meaning, and application in modern law. Present a case study where the maxim was applied.

2. Analyze a Judgment for Legal Maxims:

Select a recent Supreme Court judgment and identify any legal maxims that were used in the court's reasoning. Discuss how the maxims influenced the outcome of the case.

3. Draft a Legal Argument Using Maxims:

Write a legal argument for a hypothetical case, incorporating at least two legal maxims to support your reasoning.

These exercises will help you understand the practical significance of legal maxims and their application in real-world legal contexts, preparing you for the nuanced and philosophical aspects of legal practice.

Glossary of Important Legal Terms

Understanding and mastering these terms will help you navigate legal discussions, write with clarity, and comprehend cases more effectively. Each term is followed by a brief explanation, and where applicable, examples or references to case law for further context.

Actus Reus: The physical act of committing a crime. It refers to the actual action or conduct that is prohibited by law. For example, in a case of theft, the act of taking someone else's property without consent is the **actus reus**.

Admissibility: Refers to the quality of evidence that allows it to be presented in court. If evidence is admissible, it means the judge or jury can consider it in deciding the case.

Affidavit: A written statement confirmed by oath or affirmation, used as evidence in court. For instance, a witness can provide an affidavit of their testimony if they are unable to appear in court.

Appeal: The process of asking a higher court to review the decision of a lower court. Appeals may result in the original decision being upheld, overturned, or modified.

Arraignment: A formal reading of charges in the presence of the defendant to inform them of the accusations. The defendant is then asked to enter a plea of guilty, not guilty, or no contest.

Bail: A sum of money or property deposited to the court to ensure the accused's release from custody and guarantee their appearance at future court proceedings.

Bench Trial: A trial where the judge, rather than a jury, acts as the fact-finder and renders a verdict.

Burden of Proof: The obligation to present evidence to prove one's assertion. In criminal cases, the prosecution has the burden to prove the defendant's guilt "beyond a reasonable doubt."

Causation: The legal principle that establishes a connection between the defendant's actions and the harm caused. It is crucial in tort and criminal law to prove that the defendant's act was the cause of the injury or damage.

Civil Law: A body of law that deals with private rights and remedies, as opposed to criminal law. Civil cases include disputes such as contracts, property, and family law matters.

Common Law: Law developed through court decisions and precedent rather than statutes. For example, many principles of contract and tort law are based on common law traditions.

Complaint: The initial pleading by the plaintiff in a civil case, stating the facts and legal reasons for the lawsuit.

Cross-Examination: The questioning of a witness by the opposing party, usually aimed at challenging the credibility or reliability of their testimony.

Damages: A monetary compensation awarded by the court to a person who has suffered loss or injury. Damages can be compensatory (to cover actual losses) or punitive (to punish the defendant).

De Facto: Latin for "in fact." Refers to practices or situations that exist in reality, even if not legally recognized.

De Jure: Latin for "by law." Refers to something that is legally recognized, whether or not it exists in reality.

Due Process: A fundamental legal principle that ensures fair treatment through the judicial system, including notice and the opportunity to be heard.

Equity: A branch of law that developed to address fairness and justice, especially in cases where common law might not provide a satisfactory remedy. Remedies in equity include injunctions and specific performance.

Estoppel: A legal principle that prevents a person from asserting a position or fact that is contrary to one they previously claimed, particularly if others have relied on the original position.

Evidence: Any form of proof legally presented during a trial to establish or disprove an alleged fact. Evidence can be direct (eyewitness testimony) or circumstantial (indirect evidence that implies a fact).

Felony: A serious crime punishable by imprisonment for more than one year or by death. Examples include murder, rape, and armed robbery.

Force Majeure: A contract clause that frees both parties from liability or obligation when an extraordinary event or circumstance beyond their control prevents one or both from fulfilling the contract.

Garnishment: A legal procedure where a portion of a person's wages or assets is seized to satisfy a debt or judgment.

Good Faith: The honest intention to act without taking unfair advantage or engaging in fraudulent conduct. It is required in many contracts and transactions.

Habeas Corpus: A legal action or writ that requires a person under arrest to be brought before a judge, especially to secure their release unless lawful grounds are shown for their detention.

Hearsay: A statement made outside of court that is offered as evidence to prove the truth of the matter asserted. Hearsay is generally inadmissible unless it falls under an exception.

Injunction: A court order that requires a person to do or refrain from doing specific acts. An injunction may be temporary or permanent, depending on the case.

In Loco Parentis: A legal doctrine allowing a person or entity to act in the role of a parent, usually concerning the care and protection of a child.

Interrogatories: Written questions sent by one party in a lawsuit to the opposing party as part of the pre-trial discovery process. The answers must be provided under oath.

Judgment: The final decision made by a court in a lawsuit. The judgment resolves the issues presented and determines the rights and obligations of the parties involved.

Jurisdiction: The authority given to a court or legal body to hear and decide cases. Jurisdiction can be based on geography, subject matter, or the parties involved.

Laches: A legal doctrine that bars a claim due to the plaintiff's unnecessary delay in asserting it, which has prejudiced the defendant.

Litigation: The process of taking legal action or resolving disputes through the court system.

Mens Rea: Latin for "guilty mind." It refers to the mental state or intent required to commit a crime. Without **mens rea**, a defendant may not be held criminally liable for certain offenses.

Mistrial: A trial that is invalid due to an error in the proceedings or the inability of the jury to reach a verdict.

Negligence: A failure to exercise the care that a reasonable person would in similar circumstances, resulting in harm or damage to another party. In tort law, negligence forms the basis of many claims for compensation.

Nolo Contendere: A plea by which a defendant in a criminal case neither admits nor disputes a charge, effectively accepting punishment without admitting guilt.

Obiter Dicta: Remarks made by a judge that are not necessary to the decision and therefore not legally binding as precedent. These comments are often insightful but do not hold legal authority.

Offer: A proposal by one party to another intending to create a legally binding agreement. An offer must be accepted for a contract to be formed.

Plaintiff: The person who brings a case against another in a court of law. In criminal cases, the plaintiff is often the state or government entity.

Plea Bargain: An agreement between the prosecution and the defendant where the defendant pleads guilty to a lesser charge or receives a reduced sentence in exchange for avoiding a trial.

Quid Pro Quo: Latin for "something for something." It refers to an exchange of goods or services, where one transfer is contingent upon the other.

Res Judicata: Latin for "a matter judged." Once a final judgment has been rendered in a case, the same parties cannot relitigate the same issue.

Restitution: Compensation required from a defendant to a victim for loss or injury caused by the defendant's actions.

Stare Decisis: Latin for "to stand by things decided." It refers to the doctrine of precedent, where courts follow previous decisions in similar cases to ensure consistency in the law.

Subpoena: A legal document ordering a person to attend court or produce evidence. Failure to comply with a subpoena can result in penalties.

Tort: A civil wrong that causes harm or loss to another, resulting in legal liability. Common torts include negligence, defamation, and trespass.

Trust: A legal arrangement in which one person (the trustee) holds property on behalf of another (the beneficiary).

Venue: The geographic location where a case is heard. Venue can influence the trial's logistics, including which court hears the case.

Voir Dire: The process of questioning potential jurors to determine their suitability for jury service, ensuring an impartial jury.

Writ: A formal written order issued by a court requiring a specific action, such as a **writ of habeas corpus** or a **writ of mandamus**.

List Of Commonly Used Legal Maxims

1. **A fortiori:** With stronger reason; all the more.
2. **A mensa et thoro:** From bed and board; a divorce a mensa et thoro is a legal separation without dissolution of the marriage.
3. **A mensa et thoro:** From table and bed; legal separation without divorce.
4. **Ab initio:** From the beginning; void ab initio means void from the outset.
5. **Actus reus:** Guilty act; wrongful deed.
6. **Ad hoc:** For this purpose; created or done for a particular purpose as necessary.
7. **Ad infinitum:** Forever; without limit; to infinity.
8. **Ad litem:** For the suit; appointed for the purposes of a particular lawsuit.
9. **Alibi:** Elsewhere; a defense that the accused was elsewhere.
10. **Amicus curiae:** Friend of the court; a person who is not a party to a case but offers information that bears on the case.
11. **Animus furandi:** Intent to steal; the intention to deprive the owner permanently of their property.
12. **Animus nocendi:** Intention to harm.

13. **Ante:** Before.
14. **Assumpsit:** He promised; a common law action for breach of contract.
15. **Audi alteram partem:** Hear the other side; the principle that both sides must be heard before a decision is made.
16. **Bona fide:** In good faith; genuine, real, without fraud or deceit.
17. **Caveat emptor:** Let the buyer beware; the principle that the buyer is responsible for checking the quality of goods before purchase.
18. **Caveat:** Beware; a warning.
19. **Certiorari:** To be informed of; a writ issued by a higher court to review a decision of a lower court.
20. **Corpus delicti:** Body of the crime; the elements that constitute a crime.
21. **Cui bono:** To whose benefit?; who stands to gain from a particular act or situation.
22. **De facto:** In fact; existing in fact, whether by right or not.
23. **De jure:** By law; existing by right or according to law.
24. **De minimis:** About minimal things; insignificant; trivial.
25. **Dictum:** A saying; a statement made by a judge in a case that is not essential to the decision and therefore not binding as precedent.
26. **Dictum:** A saying; a statement of opinion.
27. **Doli incapax:** Incapable of malice; a child under the age of seven is presumed incapable of committing a crime.

28. **Ejusdem generis:** Of the same kind; a rule of statutory interpretation that where general words follow specific words, the general words are limited to things of the same kind as the specific words.

29. **Ex gratia:** Out of grace; as a favor.

30. **Ex officio:** From the office; by virtue of one's position.

31. **Ex parte:** From one side; a proceeding in which only one party is present.

32. **Ex post facto:** After the fact; a law that retroactively changes legal consequences.

33. **Ex post:** After the fact; ex post facto law is a law that applies retroactively.

34. **Expressio unius est exclusio alterius:** The express mention of one thing excludes all others; a rule of statutory interpretation that the express mention of one thing implies the exclusion of others.

35. **Felo de se:** Felon of himself; suicide.

36. **Fiduciary:** A person in a position of trust and confidence.

37. **Habeas corpus:** You have the body; a writ requiring a person to be brought before a court to determine if they are being held unlawfully.

38. **Ibid:** In the same place; used in citations.

39. **Ignorantia juris non excusat:** Ignorance of the law is no excuse.

40. **In camera:** In chambers; in private, in a judge's chambers.

41. **In curia:** In court; in open court.

42. **In flagrante delicto:** In blazing offense; caught in the act of committing a crime.

43. **In limine:** At the outset; a motion made at the beginning of a trial to exclude evidence.

44. **In loco parentis:** In the place of a parent; acting as a parent.

45. **In pari delicto:** In equal fault; equally at fault.

46. **In personam:** Against the person; a lawsuit against a specific person.

47. **In rem:** Against the thing; a lawsuit against property.

48. **Inter alia:** Among other things.

49. **Intra vires:** Within the powers; within the legal authority or power of a person or body.

50. **Ipso facto:** By the fact itself; by the very nature of the thing.

51. **Juris et de jure:** Of law and from law; a conclusive presumption that cannot be rebutted.

52. **Jus cogens:** Compelling law; a peremptory norm of international law that cannot be derogated from by states.

53. **Lex fori:** Law of the forum; the law of the jurisdiction where a case is being heard.

54. **Lex loci:** Law of the place; the law of the place where an event occurred.

55. **Lis pendens:** Suit pending; a notice that a lawsuit is pending that may affect title to property.

56. **Mala fide:** In bad faith; with bad intent.

57. **Mandamus:** We command; a writ issued by a court to compel a public official to perform a legal duty.

58. **Mens rea:** Guilty mind; the mental element of a crime.

59. **Modus operandi:** Manner of operation; a method of operating.

60. **Mutatis mutandis:** With necessary changes; with the necessary changes having been made.

61. **Nemo judex in causa sua:** No one should be a judge in his own cause; the principle that a judge must be impartial.

62. **Nolle prosequi:** To be unwilling to prosecute; a decision by a prosecutor not to proceed with a case.

63. **Nolo contendere:** I do not wish to contend; a plea that does not admit guilt.

64. **Non compos mentis:** Not of sound mind; mentally incompetent.

65. **Noscitur a sociis:** It is known from its associates; a rule of statutory interpretation that the meaning of a word can be determined from the words around it.

66. **Nulla poena sine lege:** No penalty without a law; the principle that there can be no punishment for an act that was not a crime at the time it was committed.

67. **Obiter dictum:** A thing said by the way; a statement made by a judge in a case that is not essential to the decision and therefore not binding as precedent.

68. **Pari passu:** With equal step; equally, without preference.

Annexure:
Expanding Legal Vocabulary

Whether you are preparing for exams, drafting legal documents, or simply seeking to expand your command of legal terminology, these resources will guide you in your journey of lifelong learning.

Recommended Books on Legal Language

Black's Law Dictionary

- **Author: Henry Campbell Black**

Why It's Essential: The definitive legal dictionary, ***Black's Law Dictionary*** is the go-to reference for understanding the precise meanings of legal terms. It offers comprehensive definitions, historical context, and usage notes, making it invaluable for any lawyer or student.

How to Use It: Keep a copy on hand while reading case law or drafting legal documents to clarify terms and concepts.

Garner's Dictionary of Legal Usage

- **Author: Bryan A. Garner**

Why It's Essential: Written by one of the most respected experts on legal writing, this explains the proper usage of legal terms and phrases, avoiding common pitfalls. It bridges the gap between linguistic clarity and legal precision.

How to Use It: Consult this book when you are unsure about the appropriateness or correct usage of legal terminology in your writing.

Legal Writing in Plain English

- **Author: Bryan A. Garner**

Why It's Essential: Although not solely focused on vocabulary, this book provides practical advice for improving the clarity and effectiveness of legal writing, which is crucial for precise communication.

How to Use It: Use this book to enhance not just your vocabulary, but your overall writing skills, particularly when you need to simplify complex legal terms for clients or non-lawyers.

Words That Wound: Critical Race Theory, Assaultive Speech, and the First Amendment

- **Authors: Mari J. Matsuda, Charles R. Lawrence III, Richard Delgado, Kimberlé Crenshaw**

Why It's Essential: This book explores the power of language in law and society, especially in the context of harmful speech. It provides insight into how legal language interacts with issues of race, power, and social justice.

How to Use It: For students interested in constitutional law, civil rights, and critical race theory, this book expands your vocabulary related to free speech and its limits.

BONUS

Visit www.svabhava.com

You will find many enriching content and additional resources for FREE to empower your Healing Journey. Here, you'll find:

- In-depth articles and guides on personal growth and spiritual development
- Exclusive podcast episodes
- Practical tools and exercises to enhance mindfulness and well-being

Regular updates on upcoming events, workshops, and webinars

Explore these resources and many more to continue your journey towards inner enlightenment and life excellence.

About the Author

Who am I?
The Eternal Question!

In this era, I am known by the name

DHANANJAY MODGALYA

I am not merely an IITian,
nor simply an IP attorney;
Torchbearer of my lineage's light,
Dhananjay, the guide of noble order.

I am not just a Vedanta voice,
nor only versed in logic's art;

Rooted in Ayurveda's grace,
in dharma firm, I play my part.

I am not merely a pathfinder,
nor simply an orator's voice;
I carry tradition's sacred light,
ever striving as Dhananjay.

I am not solely a creator of mantras,
nor only a master of worldly knowledge;
I blend Vedanta into modern framework,
as Dhananjay, a knower of truth.

I am neither solely a mystic
nor merely wise in mantras;
Wherever there is unio n, there I stand as,
a teacher embodying reason and intellect.

I am not only a voice of Tantra
nor merely a companion of the Gita;
Nurtured by universally acclaimed Gurus,
Dhananjay, bearing the essence of values.

I am not merely on the path of enlightenment
nor solely the lord of yogic powers;
I am the essence of life's principles,
always a seeker, always Dhananjay.

I am not merely a traveler of duties
nor simply one bound by steps;
I am the doer aligned with svabhava,
Dhananjay, united with all beings.

नाहं केवलं पथिकः कर्तव्येषु,
नाहं केवलं गमनान्तनिर्मितः।

सर्वस्वभाव सिद्धानन्दकर्मा,
धनञ्जयोऽस्मि सर्वात्मसङ्गः॥

To know more and learn more connect with me:

https://dhananjaymodgalya.com

https://svabhava.com

Email: peace@dhananjaymodgalya.com

सर्वेषां जीववृत्तेऽन्तः,
नित्यो नृत्यः स्वभावजः।
प्रबोधनं प्रतीक्षन्ते,
स्वभावस्य रहस्यकृत्॥

In the heart of every being
lies a unique rhythm,
A dance of 'Svabhava'
waiting to be awakened.

Thank you for reading Mastering Legal Language.

Your support means a lot!

For more Books by Dhananjay Modgalya visit:

https://www.amazon.in/stores/Dhananjay-Modgalya/author/B0BGJ9JCHG

Scan the QR code below:

Wishing you peace and blessings on your spiritual journey!

List of Cited Cases

A.K. Kraipak v. Union of India (1970): A.I.R. 1970 S.C. 150.

A.R. Antulay v. R.S. Nayak (1988): 1988 Supp. (1) S.C.R. 1; A.I.R. 1988 S.C. 1531; (1988) 2 S.C.C. 602.

A.K. Gopalan v. State of Madras (1950): A.I.R. 1950 S.C. 27.

Aadhaar Case (Justice K.S. Puttaswamy v. Union of India, 2018): (2019) 1 S.C.C. 1.

Aarushi Talwar murder case (2012): Nupur Talwar vs Cbi & Anr, 2012 (11) SCC 465

ADM Jabalpur v. Shivkant Shukla (1976): A.I.R. 1976 S.C. 1207.

Allcard v. Skinner (1887): (1887) 36 Ch. D. 145 (C.A.).

Anathula Sudhakar v. P. Buchi Reddy (2008): (2008) 4 S.C.C. 594.

Arnesh Kumar v. State of Bihar (2014): (2014) 8 S.C.C. 273.

Arun G. Hegde v. State of Karnataka (2019): N/A.

Bachan Singh v. State of Punjab (1980): (1980) 2 S.C.C. 684.

Balfour v. Balfour (1919): [1919] 2 K.B. 571 (C.A.).

Balwant Singh v. Commissioner of Police (1985): N/A.

Bank of Bihar v. State of Bihar (1972): A.I.R. 1971 S.C. 1210.

Barnett v. Chelsea and Kensington Hospital Management Committee (1969): [1969] 1 Q.B. 428.

Bhagwandas Goverdhandas Kedia v. Girdharilal Parshottamdas & Co. (1966): A.I.R. 1966 S.C. 543.

Bhagwati Developers Pvt. Ltd. v. Peerless General Finance & Investment Co. Ltd. (2013): (2013) 11 S.C.C. 572.

Bhupinder Singh v. Pritam Singh (2009): N/A.

Bird v. Jones (1845): (1845) 7 Q.B. 742.

Bishan Das v. State of Punjab (1961): A.I.R. 1961 S.C. 1570.

Bodh Raj v. State of Jammu and Kashmir (2002): (2002) 8 S.C.C. 45.

Bolton v. Stone (1951): [1951] A.C. 850 (H.L.).

Brown v. Board of Education (1954): 347 U.S. 483 (1954).

Butterfield v. Forrester (1809): 11 East 60, 103 Eng. Rep. 926 (K.B. 1809).

Caparo Industries Plc v. Dickman (1990): [1990] 2 A.C. 605 (H.L.).

Carlill v. Carbolic Smoke Ball Company (1893): [1893] 1 Q.B. 256 (C.A.).

Cartledge v. E Jopling & Sons Ltd (1963): [1963] A.C. 758 (H.L.).

Celotex Corp. v. Catrett (1986): 477 U.S. 317 (1986).

Central London Property Trust Ltd v. High Trees House Ltd (1947): [1947] K.B. 130.

Chinnaya v. Ramayya (1882): ILR (1876-82) 4 Mad 137

D.K. Basu v. State of West Bengal (1997): (1997) 1 S.C.C. 416.

Dahlia v. Four Millbank Nominees (1978): [1978] Ch. 231 (C.A.).

Daimler Co Ltd v. Continental Tyre and Rubber Co (Great Britain) Ltd (1916): [1916] 2 A.C. 307 (H.L.).

Delhi Development Authority v. Skipper Construction Co. (1996): (1996) 4 S.C.C. 622.

Donoghue v. Stevenson (1932): [1932] A.C. 562 (H.L.).

DPP v. Smith (1961): [1961] A.C. 290 (H.L.).

Fisher v. University of Texas (2016): 579 U.S. (2016).

Ganga Ram Moolchandani v. State of Rajasthan (2001): 2001 (6) SCC 89

Girijanandini v. Bijendra Narain (1967): 1967 SCR (1) 93

Golak Nath v. State of Punjab (1967): A.I.R. 1967 S.C. 1643.

Gorkha Security Services v. Govt of NCT of Delhi (2014): 2014 (9) SCC 105.

Grant v. Australian Knitting Mills Ltd (1936): [1936] A.C. 85 (P.C.).

Guruvayoor Devaswom Managing Committee v. Rajan (2003): 2003 (7) SCC 546.

Hadley v. Baxendale (1854): 9 Ex. 341, 156 Eng. Rep. 145 (Exch. 1854).

Hardeep Singh v. State of Punjab (2014): 2014 (3) SCC 92.

Harshad Mehta Securities Scam (1992): Ram Narain Popli vs Central Bureau Of Investigation, 2003 (3) SCC 641.

Hedley Byrne & Co Ltd v. Heller & Partners Ltd (1964): [1964] A.C. 465 (H.L.).

Hickman v. Taylor (1947): 329 U.S. 495 (1947).

Hochster v. De La Tour (1853): 2 E. & B. 678, 118 Eng. Rep. 922 (Q.B. 1853).

Home Office v. Dorset Yacht Co Ltd (1970): [1970] A.C. 1004 (H.L.).

Hussainara Khatoon v. State of Bihar (1979): A.I.R. 1979 S.C. 1369.

Hyde v. Wrench (1840): 3 Beav. 334, 49 Eng. Rep. 132 (Ch. 1840).

Indira Nehru Gandhi v. Raj Narain (1975): A.I.R. 1975 S.C. 2299.

Indra Sawhney v. Union of India (1992): A.I.R. 1993 S.C. 477.

Jessica Lal Murder Case (1999): Sidhartha Vashisht @ Manu Sharma vs State (Nct Of Delhi), 2010 (6) SCC 1.

Juggi Lal Kamlapat v. CIT (1969): 1970 SCR (1) 720.

K. Veeraswami v. Union of India (1991): 1991 S.C.C. (3) 655.

K.M. Nanavati v. State of Maharashtra (1961): A.I.R. 1962 S.C. 605.

K.S. Puttaswamy v. Union of India (2017): (2017) 10 S.C.C. 1.

K.T. Plantation Pvt. Ltd. v. State of Karnataka (2011): (2011) 9 S.C.C. 1.

Kalyani (Dead) by L.R.s v. Narayanan (1980): AIR 1980 SC 1173.

Karti P. Chidambaram v. Directorate of Enforcement (2019): AIR 2020 SC 1699.

Kesavananda Bharati v. State of Kerala (1973): A.I.R. 1973 S.C. 1461.

Keshav Singh v. Speaker, Legislative Assembly, UP (1965): A.I.R. 1965 S.C. 745.

Keshavan Madhava Menon v. State of Bombay (1951): A.I.R. 1951 S.C. 128.

Khatri v. State of Bihar (1981): A.I.R. 1981 S.C. 928.

Kochunni v. State of Madras (1960): A.I.R. 1960 S.C. 1080.

Lalita Kumari v. Govt. of Uttar Pradesh (2014): (2014) 2 S.C.C. 1.

Lillie v. Director of Public Prosecutions (2002): [2003] Crim LR 45.

Lily Thomas v. Union of India (2013): (2013) 7 S.C.C. 653.

Lily Thomas v. Union of India (2000): 2000 6 SCC 224.

M.C. Mehta v. Union of India (1987): A.I.R. 1987 S.C. 1086.

M.R. Prabhakar and Others v. Canara Bank (2012): 2012 (9) SCC 671.

Macaura v. Northern Assurance Co Ltd (1925): [1925] A.C. 619 (H.L.).

Maneka Gandhi v. Union of India (1978): A.I.R. 1978 S.C. 597; (1978) 1 S.C.C. 248.

Mapp v. Ohio (1961): 367 U.S. 643 (1961).

Maqbool Hussain v. State of Bombay (1953): A.I.R. 1953 S.C. 325.

Marbury v. Madison (1803): 5 U.S. (1 Cranch) 137 (1803).

McCulloch v. Maryland (1819): 17 U.S. (4 Wheat.) 316 (1819).

Minerva Mills v. Union of India (1980): A.I.R. 1980 S.C. 1789; (1980) 3 S.C.C. 625.

Miranda v. Arizona (1966): 384 U.S. 436 (1966).

Mohar Singh v. Devi Charan (1988): 1988 (3) SCC 63.

Mohori Bibee v. Dharmodas Ghose (1903): (1903) L.R. 30 I.A. 114 (P.C.).

Monsanto Co. v. Coramandal Indag Products (1986): A.I.R. 1986 S.C. 712.

Moti Ram v. State of Madhya Pradesh (1978): A.I.R. 1978 S.C. 1594.

N. Balakrishnan v. M. Krishnamurthy (1998): (1998) 7 S.C.C. 123.

Nandini Satpathy v. P.L. Dani (1978): A.I.R. 1978 S.C. 1025.

Narendra Singh v. State of M.P. (2004): 2004 (10) SCC 699.

Narmada Bachao Andolan v. Union of India (2000): A.I.R. 2000 S.C. 3751; (2000) 10 S.C.C. 664.

National Textile Corporation v. Nareshkumar Badrikumar Jagad (2011): AIR 2012 SC 264.

Navtej Singh Johar v. Union of India (2018): (2018) 10 S.C.C. 1.

New York Times Co. v. Sullivan (1964): 376 U.S. 254 (1964).

Nirbhaya Rape Case (2012): Mukesh & Anr. v. State for NCT of Delhi & Ors., (2017) 6 S.C.C. 1.

O.J. Simpson trial (1995): People v. Simpson, 1995 WL 135109 (L.A. Ct. Super. 1995).

Olga Tellis v. Bombay Municipal Corporation (1985): A.I.R. 1986 S.C. 180.

Overseas Tankship (U.K.) Ltd v. Morts Dock and Engineering Co Ltd (The Wagon Mound) (1961): [1961] A.C. 388 (P.C.).

P. Nalla Thampy v. B. L. Show (1974): 1984 AIR 135.

P.A. Inamdar v. State of Maharashtra (2005): (2005) 6 S.C.C. 537.

P.C. Cheriyan v. Mst. Barfi Devi (1980): A.I.R. 1980 S.C. 86.

Pakala Narayana Swami v. Emperor (1939): [1939] U.K.P.C. 21; (1939) L.R. 66 I.A. 66.

Panchdeo Narain Srivastava v. Km. Jyoti Sahay (1983): A.I.R. 1983 S.C. 462.

Paris v. Stepney Borough Council (1951): [1951] A.C. 367 (H.L.).

Pharmaceutical Society of Great Britain v. Boots Cash Chemists (Southern) Ltd (1953): [1953] 1 Q.B. 401 (C.A.).

Plessy v. Ferguson (1896): 163 U.S. 537 (1896).

Priyanka Srivastava v. State of Uttar Pradesh (2015): (2015) 6 S.C.C. 287.

Queen Empress v. Abdullah (1885): I.L.R. 7 All. 385.

R (on the application of Miller) v. Secretary of State for Exiting the European Union (2017): [2017] UKSC 5; [2017] 2 W.L.R. 583.

R v. Christie (1914): [1914] A.C. 545 (H.L.).

R v. Cunningham (1957): [1957] 2 Q.B. 396 (C.A.).

R v. Dudley and Stephens (1884): 14 Q.B.D. 273 (Q.B.).

R v. Latimer (1886): 17 Q.B.D. 359 (C.C.R.).

R v. Pagett (1983): (1983) 76 Cr. App. R. 279 (C.A.).

R v. Ratten (1972): [1972] A.C. 378 (P.C.).

R v. Sussex Justices, ex parte McCarthy (1924): [1924] 1 K.B. 256 (K.B.).

R v. White (1910): [1910] 2 K.B. 124 (C.C.R.).

R v. Venna (1976): [1976] Q.B. 421 (C.A.).

Ram Chandra v. Municipal Corporation of Delhi (1989): A.I.R. 1989 S.C. 1176.

Ranganayakamma v. Alwar Setti (1889): I.L.R. 13 Mad. 214.

Re McArdle (1951): [1951] Ch. 669 (C.A.).

Regents of the University of California v. Bakke (1978): 438 U.S. 265 (1978)

Ridge v. Baldwin (1964): [1964] A.C. 40 (H.L.).

Robinson v. California (1962): 370 U.S. 660 (1962).

Roe v. Wade (1973): 410 U.S. 113 (1973).

Rohtas Bhivaji Patil v. Assistant Collector (1991): A.I.R. 1991 S.C. 787.

Rookes v. Barnard (1964): [1964] A.C. 1129 (H.L.).

Royal British Bank v. Turquand (1856): 6 E. & B. 327; 119 Eng. Rep. 886 (Exch. Ch.).

Rylands v. Fletcher (1868): L.R. 3 H.L. 330.

S. Rangarajan v. P. Jagjivan Ram (1989): A.I.R. 1989 S.C. 2193.

S.P. Gupta v. Union of India (1981): A.I.R. 1982 S.C. 149.

S.R. Bommai v. Union of India (1994): A.I.R. 1994 S.C. 1918.

Salomon v. A. Salomon & Co. Ltd. (1897): [1897] A.C. 22 (H.L.).

Sanjeev Kumar v. State of Haryana (2020): (2020) 3 S.C.C. 394.

Shanti Devi v. Amal Kumar Banerjee (1981): A.I.R. 1981 S.C. 1550.

Shayara Bano v. Union of India (2017): (2017) 9 S.C.C. 1.

Sheela Barse v. Union of India (1986): A.I.R. 1986 S.C. 1773.

Shyam Sundar v. State of Rajasthan (1974): A.I.R. 1974 S.C. 890.

Siddharam Satlingappa Mhetre v. State of Maharashtra (2010): (2011) 1 S.C.C. 694.

Smith v. Baker (1891): [1891] A.C. 325 (H.L.).

Spiliada Maritime Corp v. Cansulex Ltd (1987): [1987] A.C. 460 (H.L.).

Standard Chartered Bank v. Directorate of Enforcement (2005): (2006) 4 S.C.C. 278.

State Bank of India v. Shyama Devi (1978): A.I.R. 1978 S.C. 1263.

State of Bihar v. Kameshwar Singh (1952): A.I.R. 1952 S.C. 252.

State of Gujarat v. Shantilal Mangaldas (1969): A.I.R. 1969 S.C. 634.

State of Kerala v. Rajesh (2020): (2020) 12 S.C.C. 122.

State of Maharashtra v. Afzal Khan (1997): A.I.R. 1997 S.C. 1.

State of Maharashtra v. M.H. Shah (1995): (1995) 5 S.C.C. 423.

State of Maharashtra v. Mohd. Yakub (1980): A.I.R. 1980 S.C. 1111.

State of Maharashtra v. Praful B Desai (2003): (2003) 4 S.C.C. 601.

State of Maharashtra v. Sukhdeo Singh (1992): (1992) 3 S.C.C. 700.

State of Maharashtra v. Suresh (2000): (2000) 1 S.C.C. 471.

State of Rajasthan v. Shera Ram (2011): (2012) 1 S.C.C. 602.

State of Rajasthan v. Union of India (1977): A.I.R. 1977 S.C. 1361.

State of Tamil Nadu v. K. Balu (2017): (2017) 2 S.C.C. 281.

State of U.P. v. Raj Narain (1975): A.I.R. 1975 S.C. 865.

State of Uttar Pradesh v. Ashok Kumar Srivastava (1992): (1992) 1 S.C.C. 107.

State of Uttar Pradesh v. Poosu (1976): A.I.R. 1976 S.C. 1750.

State of Uttar Pradesh v. Singhara Singh (1964): A.I.R. 1964 S.C. 358.

State of West Bengal v. Anwar Ali Sarkar (1952): A.I.R. 1952 S.C. 75.

State of West Bengal v. S.K. Ghosh: A.I.R. 1963 S.C. 255.

State of West Bengal v. Shew Mangal Singh (1981): A.I.R. 1981 S.C. 1917.

State v. Afzal Guru (2005): (2005) 11 S.C.C. 760.

State v. Sanjay Dutt (1993): (1994) 5 S.C.C. 410.

Subramanian v. Public Prosecutor (1956): [1956] 1 W.L.R. 965 (P.C.).

Sunil Batra v. Delhi Administration (1978): A.I.R. 1978 S.C. 1675.

Suresh Jindal v. State of Delhi (2001): (2001) 3 S.C.C. 673.

Suresh Kumar Koushal v. Naz Foundation (2013): (2014) 1 S.C.C. 1.

Swami Motors v. Ashok Leyland Ltd. (1997): A.I.R. 1997 S.C. 2793.

T.N. Godavarman Thirumulpad v. Union of India (1997): (1997) 2 S.C.C. 267.

Tata Cellular v. Union of India (1994): (1994) 6 S.C.C. 651.

Tata Consultancy Services v. Cyrus Mistry (2021): (2021) 9 S.C.C. 449.

Tata Tea v. SEC of India (2001): (2001) 2 S.C.C. 224.

Taylor v. Caldwell (1863): 3 B. & S. 826, 122 Eng. Rep. 309 (K.B.).

Thabo Meli v. R (1954): [1954] 1 W.L.R. 228 (P.C.).

The Ayodhya Dispute (2019): *M. Siddiq (D) Thr Lrs v. Mahant Suresh Das & Ors.*, (2019) 15 S.C.C. 1.

Tukaram v. State of Maharashtra (1979): A.I.R. 1979 S.C. 185.

Tulk v. Moxhay (1848): 2 Ph. 774, 41 Eng. Rep. 1143 (Ch.).

Union Carbide Corporation v. Union of India (1989): A.I.R. 1990 S.C. 273.

United States v. Marion (1971): 404 U.S. 307 (1971).

United States v. Nixon (1974): 418 U.S. 683 (1974).

Vaughan v. Taff Vale Railway Co. (1860): 5 H. & N. 679, 157 Eng. Rep. 1351 (Exch.).

Vishaka v. State of Rajasthan (1997): A.I.R. 1997 S.C. 3011.

Vishwanath v. State of Uttar Pradesh (1960): A.I.R. 1960 S.C. 67.

Vodafone India v. Union of India (2012): (2012) 6 S.C.C. 613.

Wooldridge v. Sumner (1963): [1963] 2 Q.B. 43 (C.A.).

Woollin v. DPP (1999): [1999] A.C. 82 (H.L.).

Woolmington v. Director of Public Prosecutions (1935): [1935] A.C. 462 (H.L.).

Books By Author

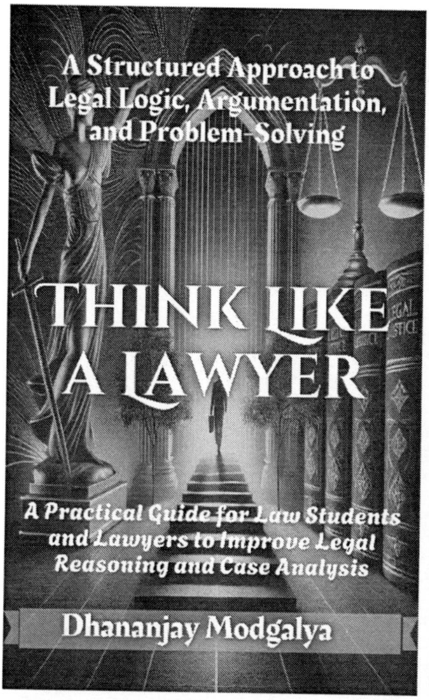

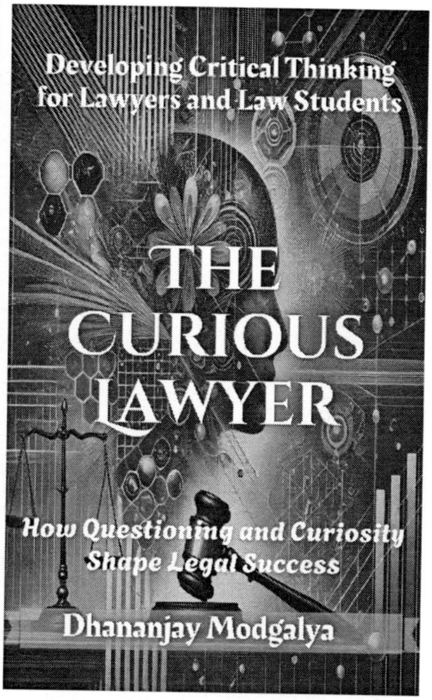